William Morse Cole

An Old Man's Romance

A Tale

William Morse Cole

An Old Man's Romance
A Tale

ISBN/EAN: 9783744692212

Printed in Europe, USA, Canada, Australia, Japan

Cover: Foto ©Thomas Meinert / pixelio.de

More available books at **www.hansebooks.com**

AN

OLD MAN'S ROMANCE

A TALE

Written by CHRISTOPHER CRAIGIE

SICUT LILIUM

INTER SPINAS

BOSTON

Published by *Copeland and Day*

MDCCCXCV

INTRODUCTORY.

HIGHBANK is unknown outside of New England, and to most New Englanders it is but a name. To a few it is a synonym for what is best in New England rural life, — the strength without the hardness of Puritanism, the earnestness without the impatience of the Western spirit, the spirituality without the coldness of Old World culture. The town boasts that most of the inhabitants were born there; and the boast might have been made at any time in the last hundred years. It boasts that it has yet to see its first factory, its first electric street-car, and its first Sunday paper. I do not need to describe its streets; for every large New England village which makes these boasts has its old but neat white houses, its newer but not staring brown houses, its capacious lawns, its shaded sidewalks, and its small but wholly trustworthy shops.

1

Many even of those who lay no claim to residence there, either past or present, cherish the town's honor almost as carefully as those whose names appear, with antique spelling, on the first tax-roll. Some of us steal away to Highbank two or three times a year to breathe its atmosphere. Nature never built a town, they say; she does n't drive thorns into her own flesh. Yet one can almost fancy that she looked on complacently when Highbank was built. Run out there from the city some day, — it does n't matter what the weather is, — and you will feel a new vigor in your breast. You will not be assailed at every turn, or at any turn, by the evidence of machinery, — mammoth, box-like buildings, smoking chimneys, wheezing engines, buzzing wheels, rattling looms, dangling wires. Best of all, the men you will meet are not machines. They are not turned out of bed by alarm-clocks; fed with steam-cooked food; whisked to business in crowded, noisy electric or elevated cars; wound up for the day's work by the sight of big machines and piles of raw material, or by

2

the morning's mail; regulated by the " Express and Shipping Guide," or the post-office schedule of mail departures; hurried through dinner by the amusement column of the evening paper; and finally sent to bed by the fear of the morning's inexorable alarm-clock.

In Highbank, the sun shines into our windows and kisses our eyes, the robin's note kisses our ears, and we wake. We look out of the window, and over our neighbor's lawn we see the valley of the river; and beyond we see old Saddleback, ready to be mounted by any restless spirit. We step out upon the grass, and let the dew take off the hideous, staring gloss which the modern shoe-blacking has given our shoes. Betty soon serves breakfast in the big, low-studded dining-room. The sun streams in through the row of eastern windows, touches the glass on the table, and fills the room with rainbows. By and by we stroll out to work. We need no stimulus. Whether or not one is lazy, the eager blood, which air and light have quickened, cries for work to do. To be sure, we do not fancy dictating the price of cotton cloth or patent-leather shoes to our type-writer, nor do we fancy taking places at rattling, greasy machines; but we feel like wielding an axe for a half-day, and guiding a plough or working at a forge for another half-day. We want to work in sight of the wide sky and open fields; and we must have work that leaves our fancy sometimes free. We scorn to bind our thought continuously to money-getting. The realm of thought is our great birthright. Shall one make a draught-horse of one's brains for a mess of pottage? When the day is done, it is our muscles, not our brains, that are tired. A quiet dinner, free from bustling waiters, from the rumble of carriages along the pavement, and from the thought of timed engagements, begins the evening. We take our books, or chat with each other or a visitor, while the girls at the piano open vistas of dreamland or memory-land to our inner eyes.

It was through my love for Highbank that I was put in the way of learning one of its romances. A serious fall in the woods on Saddleback forced me to spend a few weeks in the Highbank hospital, healing a broken leg. My nearest neighbor was an old gentleman of seventy, or thereabouts, who had received internal injuries in a railway accident. As he did not leave his room, it was not until I was allowed to wheel myself about in an invalid's chair that I came to know him. Then out of our common love for the town grew a considerable intimacy.

He was a thoroughly lovable old man. He had preserved his powers in an uncommon degree. The only sign of age was a certain timidity; yet I doubt whether, in thought, at least, the seeming timidity was more than a natural conservatism. At any rate, he had even less of it than is common among professional and business men of his age.

He spent much of his time in writing. One day, on learning that he had been for many years engaged in work of a literary nature, I ventured to ask him whether he had an unfinished book on hand.

"No," he said, "I am writing for wholly personal reasons. I am trying to picture one side of my life as it has been during the last few years. I am trying to show how another life has touched my old age, and made it joyful."

His answer keenly aroused my curiosity. Two young people were in almost constant attendance upon him, and I was eager to know whether either of them was the person whose influence had been so happy. One was a young man, about twenty-two years old, with athletic figure, ruddy cheeks, and laughing blue eyes. It was hard to look into his face without smiling in sympathy with his thorough boyishness. He was one of those who take life to be just what it seems on its face to be. The other visitor was a young woman, of perhaps twenty, tall and slight. Her features were not exactly regular, — surely not classical. I doubt whether any one who had studied her face would call her handsome, or even pretty. One would not ask whether she were either; one did not care, — she was so much better than either. Beautiful was the word for it. The charm came from within.

6

"In view of the trouble your injured side gives you, I must say that I admire your diligence," I answered.

"I don't mind that. My task is worth while. A young girl, whom you know, has been a great joy to me. Her power for either good or evil in the world is almost infinite. I have known her well, and I want her to see herself as I see her. So I am attempting to tell the story of her part in my life. I mean to show her the story some day."

Soon after, his eyes failed him; and I became his amanuensis. He had already carried the outline of the story to the point where it became a journal, but in many parts it was still fragmentary. We went back to pick up the dropped threads, and meanwhile the journal was neglected. I witnessed, however, the last scenes of the story, and thus can fill out the unfinished manuscript.

The time has come when it may be made public without annoyance to any one. Only a change of names is necessary.

I.

AS I lie and listen to approaching and retiring footsteps in the corridor, I cannot help wondering at the strange turn of fate which has brought me here. The dearest place on earth is the place where one has felt the deepest passion, whether of joy or of sorrow. How strange that, though I have wandered for forty years, I was in Highbank when fate struck me down, and left me with nothing to do but to dream! Here I lived my short season of buoyant joy; here I suffered; and here began, long years after, a new life, which was neither joy nor sorrow, but strangely compounded of both. Indeed, in this new life I have lived over the old life, — but only as autumn echoes spring.

Strangely, from my window I can see the street corner where, nine years ago, the new life began.

The day was clear and stingingly cold. The hard-packed snow upon the sidewalk rang at every blow. The afternoon schools had just closed, and the children were flocking home. I often say that if one will show me the children of a town, I can tell at once the character of the people. Wherever I go, I watch for them. Those of Highbank have always had great interest for me. I have often wondered whether they are unusually interesting in themselves, or whether the fact that I was once one of them, and love the town, makes me love them. As I stood waiting on the sidewalk, I watched the group of girls approaching me. I had just returned to Highbank after an absence of ten years, and I was eager to see the new generation. In the group were several attractive faces. One, in particular, held my attention. The child was about twelve years old, but tall for her age; she was slight, and as straight as an Indian, but so well poised and so graceful in every step and turn that one would instinctively liken her to a bird. Her features were not regular, according to recognized standards; but by so much the more was the information which they gave about her character positive. Every line meant something. Her mouth was large, and the lips, though full, were firm and free from any suggestion of too ruddy coloring; her eyes were a deep blue. As she passed me, they were kindled by an eager light of sympathy with a companion's evident happiness.

Several of the girls were talking at once, as girls will, and none of them particularly noticed a small colored boy trudging along with a big basket on a sled. As they passed, the boy pulled the sled a little to one side in order to give more room, and in doing so slipped and fell. In striking the sidewalk, he hurt his hand. He lay there, crying softly, to nurse it. The girl who had interested me was in the front of the group, and did not see the fall. A half-smothered exclamation of pity from one of the others must have caught her ear after they had passed, for she turned suddenly about, looked back, and then came running, with face radiant with sympathy. I had in the mean time approached near enough to see the tenderness of her beautiful eyes as she took the boy's bare little hand in her own mittened one. It was hard to believe that he was not shivering. His clothes not only were thin and ragged, but they hung upon him so loosely that it was doubtful whether he had comfortable underwear beneath. In a moment he was nestled upon the top of the basket, with his hands buried in the girl's muff. In another moment she had taken the sled-rope, and he was spinning over the snow. His white teeth, shining between his laughing lips, belied the freezing tears upon his sleeve. The bruised and tingling fingers were forgotten.

I followed the gay party. Much to my surprise and pleasure, when the boy had been sent on his way happy, the girl entered the house of an old friend, Arthur Thomas, upon whom I was intending to call in the evening.

II.

WHEN I was ushered into my friend's library, I found the child whom I had seen in the afternoon, reading before the open fire. She rose as I entered, and asked me whether I wished to see her uncle.

"Yes," I answered; "but I am very glad to see you, too, though I fancy you don't know that you ever saw me before."

"No, sir," she replied; "I don't think I ever have. Have I?"

"I am not sure. At any rate, I have seen you before, although I am a stranger in town, — at least, I call myself a stranger here nowadays."

"I can't imagine where you have seen me, sir."

"Not long ago," I replied, "I saw one of a group of school-girls leave her companions, and after lending her muff to a ragged, shivering negro boy, give him a ride. Did you ever know of a case like that?"

"But I should n't think you would remember me."

"I try always to remember people who do that sort of thing."

Arthur came in, and the child started to go. He stopped her; and after introducing her as his niece, Ruth, he told her that since her own room was not warm enough for reading, she would better stay in the library. She went back to her book, and my friend and I talked over the changes in town and people during the thirty years since I had first left it. As he was several years younger than I, the Highbank even of his boyhood was different from that of mine; and he had watched all the changes of later years.

Arthur soon left the room to hunt up some old maps, and I found an object of absorbing interest in the face by the fireside. The child was reading intently, and could not know that I was watching her. I had never before so much regretted that I was not an artist. In the deep blue eyes, the fair brow, the brown hair, and the rich coloring and delicate shading of abound-

13

ing health in the cheeks, one saw the essential quality of all beauty. As in a summer sunrise, the material, earthly though it was, transcended itself and told only of the ethereal. No slightest blemish or crude outline reminded of the trammels of the flesh. The physical was there only to translate the spirituality into earthly life.

As I watched, a smile played about her lips; and then a convulsive shrug of the shoulders told of the laugh which is half of humor, half of sympathy. In another moment tears suffused her eyes, and she threw up her head to look at the ceiling until they should go. She soon returned to her book; but before she turned the page, a convulsive, half-stifled sob stopped the reading. When she noticed that I was watching her, the color rose to her face, and she closed the book.

"Have you finished your book?" I asked.

"No, sir; not quite."

"I should n't think you would want to stop, then; for it seems very interesting."

She made no response.

"Is your book sad?" I asked.

"No, sir; not especially."

"You make me very curious, you see. The story must have been a true one."

"No, sir; I don't think it is."

I felt that fear of showing too much feeling before a stranger had brought the reading to so sudden a close. I was curious to draw her out, and to see in what spirit she did her reading. I looked at her face again carefully before venturing with my next remark.

"Some people, you know, say that it is foolish to laugh and cry with the heroes and heroines of stories. They ask why we should care about things that never really happened."

"I don't know whether I ever thought of it before," she said. She put her hand to her forehead for a moment, as if she had been asked a puzzling question in school. I began to wish that I had not carried her the suggestion. "Isn't it well," she asked at last, hesitatingly, "to be moved by any beautiful thing, even if it's only the thought of some one who writes stories? I don't know about the sad parts,

15

though, — whether it is n't foolish to cry over them — unless — unless somehow it does our hearts good and makes them more tender to have sympathy with real trouble."

" You have given a pretty good answer to the critics. As you grow older, you will probably realize it more and more. I think likely that you had been reading about some kind-hearted person just before you helped that little negro boy this afternoon."

" I don't think that was very kind," she answered, with a pleased smile and a faint blush; " I enjoyed it as much as he did."

" It was all the kinder of you to do it without stopping to think whether it was kind or not. You can make a great many people happy in a lifetime, if you are always as eager to help."

" I 'm sure it is n't hard to do that sort of thing," was the simple reply.

Arthur now returned with the maps. Soon Ruth went off to bed. When she had gone, I asked about her.

" She is the orphaned daughter of my wife's sister," he replied. " Mrs. Thomas and I wish to keep her with us, but the other branches of the family insist on having her with them a part' of every year. As a result, the poor child has no home, — or, rather, has several homes. We do not have very much of her; for Mrs. Thomas was much younger than Ruth's mother, and the older aunts insist that they have stronger claims to her. Everybody wants her. She comes to us as a godsend; and when she leaves us, we begin to look forward to her coming back. I can't help loving her almost as if she were my own. I can hardly believe that a child of my own would be so thoroughly lovable."

On the last day of my stay in Highbank, I wandered out to Black Pond, which had been from time immemorial the favorite skating-ground of the town. The day was clear and very cold, but the air was dry. It was such a day that one's body seemed meant to soar, and one became impatient because something — one hardly knew what — kept one tied to earth. I could not resist the temptation to try skates once more. I knew that people would be inclined to laugh at an old man on skates; but I have a theory that the best way to keep from growing old is to keep up the wise interests of youth.

As I skated toward the secluded cove where I once learned to make the figure eight on skates, I passed a group of girls who seemed to find it hard to play their game of tag in harmony. One was asserting, in a loud and peevish tone, that she had tagged another, and the other was strenuously denying it. So violent was the quarrel that if the players had been boys I should have looked for blows. The dispute was finally settled, but the sullen looks remained.

When I reached the entrance of the cove, I found three girls in possession. Two were standing still, watching the third. Few people were near that part of the pond, and the young skater had abandoned herself to the whim of the moment. I had never before known a woman or girl to have such mastery over skates. You have seen a dog on a joyous summer day running across the fields with all his might, darting into a thicket, jumping over a stream, chasing a bird, leaping at a butterfly, and then bounding back to his master, only to bound off again and repeat it all. The same healthy, passionate joy in mere existence seemed to move in the young girl's muscles. Rolls and spins and changes of edge succeeded each other in rapid succession. Now and then a graceful little leap seemed to launch her spirit away from all limitations of the body into the air, as a bird sent out with a joyous message. I entered the cove as soon as she stopped. Her eyes, her cheeks, the very pose of her body, spoke of thrilled energy. When I had approached, I saw that it was my friend's niece.

"Ah, my dear," said I, "I wish you had been like this when I was a boy. This was my favorite cove, and many a trick I practised here; but I never learned to do any of them better than you did just now. I would have given a good deal, forty or fifty years ago, for a girl companion who could skate like that."

"I thought no one would see me here," she answered with a smile. "Auntie says it is n't nice for girls to skate so freely in public; it attracts attention. I don't mean," she added hastily, "that my skating was good enough to attract attention, for I know it was n't; but people are n't used to seeing girls hop about so freely on skates, and so might think that I liked to attract notice."

"I can't say that your aunt is wrong on general principles; but surely there can be no harm in your skating as freely as you like in this secluded place. It could do no harm if a few people did see you; it would only cheer them up and put new life into them as it did into me. Won't you skate once round the pond with me? Perhaps, then, I can catch something of your inspiration."

Though her exercise had been violent and long continued, her hand was firm, and her stroke showed none of the unsteadiness of knee and ankle which the exhausted skater tries in vain to conceal.

When we reached the group of girls who were playing tag, another dispute was in progress. Ruth excused herself on the ground that she had promised to join the game after a few moments of skating in the cove. Her coming was greeted with cries of "Here's Ruth; we 'll leave it to her!" The question seemed a knotty one. The solution was original; I suspected that it was characteristic of the solver.

"I can't decide it, girls," she exclaimed after a few moments of puzzling. "I'll be 'it' myself; that's the easiest way to settle it."

With a smiling face she started after the best skaters, leaving the smaller girls and the poorer skaters opportunity to escape. I watched the group for a long time, but I heard no more disputes. Once the situation was critical, but a word turned it.

"What's the use of getting angry?" I heard her say; "you'll have to get over it, and that's what hurts the most."

The girls laughed, and good-nature was restored.

Most of the skaters walked back to town. I was glad to find a place in the middle of the line. Few companies suggest pleasanter things than a homeward-bound skating-party at tea-time,—the afternoon of sport, the invigoration of spirit following from the tiring of the muscles, the cheerful home tea-table, where one finds, not only the reality of what hunger already sees in vision, but willing ears for eager lips to fill with a day's experiences.

I was much interested in the talk of two boys behind me; evidently something had gone wrong in school. I could make out only that one of the girls had been sent home for insubordination, and that some of the scholars took her part and others condemned her.

When the boys turned the corner, I slackened my pace in the hope that another interesting couple would come within hearing. I had not long to wait. It happened, however, that Ruth came up behind me, and I did not feel justified in lagging and overhearing the conversation. I caught only a word now and then, sometimes in her voice, sometimes in that of a boy of fifteen or thereabouts, and occasionally I heard her light laugh. Just before we reached the town, they passed me, and I heard her words.

"I don't care," she was saying; "I don't believe there is any sense in what Miss Paterson wanted me to do. Uncle Arthur said he could n't understand what good it could do.

I don't intend to waste my time in that way; they may suspend me if they like, or even expel me. I suppose it's an awful thing for a girl to be expelled from school; but I said I wouldn't do that work until I saw some reason for it, and I won't. Miss Paterson refuses to give any sensible reason, and that's the end of it. I suppose it's very wicked, but I can't help it. They may punish me — "

I heard no more. The next day I left Highbank.

III.

IT is strange that for years our eyes will remain closed to some one or more of the best interests of life. Sometimes, after years of blindness, a chance opens them suddenly. I found in my friend's niece something which threw new light on young girls. In my eyes they suddenly became interesting. Few men go through life without a season of interest in girlhood. Some have it early; but then it is almost sure, to use a university phrase, to turn to specialization, and become worse than useless. Others have it late, and soon outgrow it; or rather, should I not say, grow away from it, for is there such a thing as growing above it? As the years had gone on with me, and I had become a confirmed bachelor, girls became more and more foreign to my life. I had known the children of my friends; but when these had grown to be men and women, I knew no children. One really knows but two generations besides one's own,—the one above and the one below. We are not likely to be quite in touch with the second remove.

What little I saw of my friend's niece taught me that I had for years closed my eyes to perhaps the most interesting phase of human development,—that from girlhood to womanhood. Suddenly I found that my eyes were invariably caught by a braid of girlish hair. So it must be with any man when his eyes are opened. The braid is the sign of almost all that is unlike himself. The horizon that its wearer knows is so small, and perchance so clear, so beautiful! She knows a mother's and a father's tender love, and the no less tender but disguised love of a tormenting brother or sister; she fancies that her friends are true to her; duty is clear,—'t is nothing more nor less than obedience to parents and the love of God; her castles in the air are so bright that it matters little that they lack definition; she fancies the love of husband and of children coming to round out the love she already knows; and she fancies that they come as calmly, unquestioned and unquestionable.

Her horizon is the horizon of day, — all, even in the far distance, is calm, clear-cut, comprehensible. And we whose horizon is that of night, we who look on and on and on and see myriads of stars, driven by immutable, awful powers, coming whence and bound whither we know not, in distances unimaginable, — we see that neat braid, swaying with the free girlish gait, and we hold our breaths in reverence. What a sacred thing is that innocence! What a curse must be upon one who breaks it rudely, thrusting the child out suddenly into the black unknown! She will be so terrified until her eyes become used to the darkness, and she can discern the outstretched light of companionship even in those unknown stars, and can feel the unity in all!

In the years following my visit to Highbank, I had good opportunity to study girls' faces, and to watch their inner development. In order to have access in my leisure to certain historical documents, I had taken up my residence in Madawanipee, — one of the few New England cities wise enough to keep its Indian name. I soon learned that Madawanipee was justly noted, not only for the excess of the feminine element in its population, but for the attractiveness of that element.

It was by good fortune that I was received on familiar terms in several families where the children were growing into manhood and womanhood. I came suddenly to realize how empty was the solitude which had of late years marked my way of living. Family life came to have its old meaning, — the meaning which made so much of the food of my dreams in youth.

Yet, though I was a privileged guest in several homes, I found that I was permitted to taste the sorrows rather than the joys of parental care. The children, of course, could make little room in their hearts for the elderly stranger; and yet my share in the parental solicitude and sorrow, as the young people grew up into broader fields and away from the old paths, was large.

Thanksgiving Day of my eighth winter in Madawanipee was somehow particularly depressing. Everywhere about me families were gathered together, and most of my older friends had not only children, but grandchildren, at their tables. My nephew, Harry Templeman, who was my only near kin, was visiting in another city. I dined alone. The evening I spent in alternately cherishing and banishing the memory of youthful days and youthful dreams in Highbank.

I devoted the following day to searching old records at the Court House. I did not care to trust my spirits to less absorbing work.

At three o'clock I congratulated myself that my plans for the day had been well laid; for success had followed them, and I had almost outlived the depression of yesterday. Never was a clearer line of descent shown in deeds and wills than that which I had traced from John Chambers of Sagadahoc, yeoman, son of Thomas Chambers of England, owner and cultivator of certain lands in Massachusetts Bay Colony in 1643. An important link in the historical chain which I was tracing had been found. My work was progressing rapidly in its last stages.

The sun broke out from the clouds, and I looked up from the yellow manuscript to watch the floating cloud-shadows on the hill-tops. The window chanced to be open, and the breeze came gently in and waved my hair. When it ceased, the loosened locks fell down over my forehead, playfully. A zephyr came in, and pushed the hair back. It went, and came again like a woman's fond hand, disarranging and rearranging, every touch a caress. My thoughts ran back many years to the hand which I used to dream would some day rest upon my brow.

The zephyr quickened to a breeze, and the breeze to a gust of wind. A dozen pages of the manuscript volume before me blew over. When I put the dream aside and looked down at my book, my eye fell on the name of John Chambers, formerly of Falmouth, England, son of Thomas Chambers, of Falmouth, an immigrant on the ship "Anne" in 1647. The context showed clearly that this was the man whose line I sought to trace. Yet neither John Chambers of Sagadahoc nor any of his descendants had returned to England, and none of his ancestors had come from Falmouth. There had been two men named John Chambers in the same neighborhood, of about the same age, sons of fathers named Thomas. Months of labor had been spent on the genealogy of the wrong family.

The winter afternoon was nearly over; it was too late to begin a new search. Indeed, I was hardly in the mood for it. It seemed as if nothing that I had ever done or attempted to do was a success. At such times one forgets one's triumphs, especially the things that the world calls triumphs and one's own ambition calls mere make-shifts. I put my papers back into their places and started out to get a little freshness from Nature, if she had any to offer. I struck out of town at random; I forgot that I had started out after freshness. I forgot that I had ever had any freshness in my life; perhaps it was true that I had not had much. At all events, it was true that none had been thrust in my way; what I had found had been eagerly sought. It had been a part of my philosophy that life was not only accidentally, but essentially, beautiful; and I had persisted in finding that beauty everywhere. Some of my friends had told me that I forced my imagination to see beauty where there was none. But to-night I gave up, for once, the quest for beauty. Was it not time that life placed some in my way?

About seven o'clock I passed over Promon-tory Hill on my way back to town. I had no special reason for going back, nor any reason for going on; I was in the mood in which one has no motive for anything. The lights of the town came into view. There is, at the same time, a singular companionship and a singular isolation in village lights at evening. The blank stare of straight walls and glistening windows is gone; the walls have relaxed their features into the quieter, mobile lines of night; each visible window tells some story, — the story of a group, or of some lonely one, near by. In the out-lying cottages of the town, the lights were few. As I passed the first, the rays streamed through a small hole in the curtain upon my path. In

31

fancy I could see the group gathered about the recently cleared dining-table within.

The father, in his shirt-sleeves, or, more likely, in his jumper, sits in a rocking-chair with his weekly paper spread out before him. One slipper has been kicked off, and lies upside down near his chair. Now and then he stretches out the slipperless foot and strokes the dog which lies under the table. Occasionally he makes a brief comment upon the news of the week, or asks one of the children where is Curaçoa, or Heligoland, or Bucharest. A girl of twelve is scanning an arithmetic placed on the table before her. The baby wants a drink of water, and while she gets it for him, the boys take her place near the lamp. When she comes back, her face falls a bit, hardens, brightens again; and without complaint she takes a poorer place, further from the light. The boys are leaning on opposite corners of their chair, with elbows on the table, chins in hand, eagerly discussing the new "St. Nicholas" or "Youth's Companion." The patient, tired-faced, but ready-hearted mother is at her mending. When the last stocking is put aside, a pair of tiny pants in the making takes its place. Long after the children have gone to bed, the needle will fly. Yet, perchance, she will dip into some book for half an hour, even after the father has gone to bed.

In that single group are found the four chief types of human thought and feeling. The father has won his place in the world, humble though it is, and he foresees no evil, no new joy; he is content with the daily life of the shop and the evening group. The boys, too, are content; but theirs is the content of fearless hopefulness. For them there is no past, and the future has no fears; they do not even prepare for it. The day's lessons are learned, or half-learned, and there's the end of it; the future will take care of the tasks of the future, and the word "fail" does not enter, even indirectly, into their forecasts. The mother's place in the world, like the father's, has been won; but it is not joyous. Her work, so nearly infinite, is never done, because strength is finite; yet her responsibility for the children is even more nearly infinite.

33

She longs for time and knowledge to look into the broader world of art and music and literature, that she may open the children's eyes; but they must be first fed and clothed, and time— oh, time! And so her life is one of thoughtlessness of the future for self, but wholly in the future for her children. The daughter is not easy-going, like the boys; she, too, dreams,— perhaps more than they,—but her dreams rest so much more on contingencies. See the determination with which she works at her arithmetic,—perchance the weariest work she ever did. Life is a bigger word with her than with any of the others. Nature made her with so much to hope for, so little to win with!

We must hold out the hand of sympathy to each one in the group,—for the father, it is in good fellowship; for the mother, in pity and praise; for the boys, in admiration; but for the girl, in love. We cannot help it. Life is so big a thing for her, and she is so nearly powerless, unhelped, to make it what she would, that nothing less than our whole hearts is worthy of our sympathy.

Across the way, the light in the attic was a lonely one. My fancy could see the poor farmer boy who had come to the town to make his fortune. The world goes hard with him; or, perchance, goes by easily and leaves him behind. His employers are crabbed. His fellow-workmen are trashy youths about town, always intent on some supper, or smoking-party, or ball, or perhaps a flirtation with some giddy school-girl or worse. The very air they breathe seems tainted with stale tobacco-smoke, or liquor fumes, or strong perfumery from some woman's dress. The thoughts that seem to fill their heads are the sins, real or imaginary, of those they know. They boast of their own transgressions. Even if he goes to church on Sunday, he hears only of "miserable sinners, all." He has begun to wonder whether there is any virtue in the world. Is no one above suspicion? He thinks of the sweet face whose cheek he kissed the evening before he came away from home. Was she like these people he hears about? Is he alone, in all the world, hungering and thirsting after righteousness, and fighting the evil that

35

tempts? He longs to look squarely into some earnest, pure face, and hear words and see deeds that confirm his faith. Great God, he will go crazy if this unmasking of vice goes on much longer! But is it vice? Has he not mistaken what is merely not highest for what is lowest? The world cannot be all wrong! It must be he that is wrong. He will give up the old faith; he will fall into line with the world. He will go out and seek company where it may be found, perhaps for the asking, perhaps only for gold. But, oh, such company! His heart revolts. He will hold to the old faith one day more, at least. He will stay at home and read his " Othello " or " Cymbeline." Hope will not die yet!

As I went further into town, the lights became thicker, — not only because the houses were more numerous, but because they were larger. I could fancy the groups about the pianos or library-tables. I felt that if I could only look deep enough, I should find the same story told everywhere. "Hope springs eternal in the human breast." The mother, in the big house

36

over there, worries over her wayward son or her vain daughter; but she never gives up. She dreams of the time when their veiled eyes shall be open, and that dream is her life. The young people next door may be discontented, rebellious against fate; but they grind their teeth in determination, and their joy — and they will come some day to confess that it was greater than they knew — is in that determination. Perhaps the father has lost his property, and, what he really cares about, his good name is smirched. His dream, his life, is to win that name free of all reproach, and he glories in the effort.

I came into sight of my own dark window. Suppose it had been lighted and I had been sitting within, would that light tell a story of hope? Had my theory of life failed in my own case? What was I looking forward to? Would it make any difference to me, even so far as satisfaction in this life was concerned, if I died tomorrow? I loved to wander in the woods and fields, to hear the birds and see the flower-life, to encounter winds and rains and watch the changing colors, to read books and hear music;

37

but my life amounted to nothing else. I had no near kin, no near friends. No one welcomed me if I came, missed me if I went. To be sure, the little Flynns rejoiced when I left a bag of apples in my clothes-basket, and the poor consumptive boy in the next street counted the hours till my landlady should appear at his back-gate with a part of my Sunday dinner. (I always wanted my Sunday dinner large enough for two, though I never ate heartily; and as I disliked to have things wasted, I sent my surplus over to the patient.) My heart was always a bit warmed by the young Flynns' shy smiles when I saw them on the street, and by the consumptive's weekly message; but such things are not more than surface-deep. It was not I whom they thanked; it was the giver of a few trifles. That was all they knew of me. What did any one know of me? To some, I was the old man who went to the Court House for a while every day, and spent the rest of the time in the open air; to others, I was an elderly gentleman who took a little interest in the various kinds of charitable work in town; to a few, I was a tolerably entertaining, occasional evening guest; to my nephew, I was an enigma, like all other elderly men.

What could such a life as mine amount to? I was not too old to do yet some good; I could, perhaps, carry comfort or cheer to some one in shadow; could make some one's hope a reality; and so my life would mean something to the world. Yet, even then, how much would it mean to me?

I felt no satisfactory purpose for doing anything. I was too listless even to go home. I stopped under a window where I heard singing; a plaintive melody voiced the words: —

    " The night has a thousand eyes,
        And the day but one ;
      Yet the light of a whole day dies
        With the setting sun.

    " The mind has a thousand eyes,
        And the heart but one ;
      Yet the light of a whole life dies
        When love is done."

I wandered on mechanically. Yes, it was true; I could, indeed, do good in the world, and make that my life. But even in that where was satisfaction? Even virtue loses its sweetness when no one cares that we are virtuous. I might win gratitude; but was it worth while? Gratitude binds hearts closer, but it also keeps them from touching. Life is not wholly lived unless the heart is so close to another that even gratitude cannot pass between. It is not enough to find some one to serve; that some one must care that it is I who serve. I had none to care; none had ever cared.

The sky was now clear. The moon had risen above the houses, and was shedding its soft light upon the snow. The shadows of the bare trees were spread in delicate tracery over the snow-drifts; I could not help stopping to admire. The hand of man never made any-thing so beautiful. I forgot, for the moment, that I had been disconsolate. I could not help being thankful for that beauty. Then came the question: Is it like a child pleased with a toy that I thank God for this beauty, or do I thank Him for Himself? Do I love Him merely as a giver of gifts, or do I love Him for Himself? Could I offer God less than I asked for myself?

Despair had come in; but when I had come to myself there was no room for it,—hope had driven it out. I had merely forgotten, for a moment, how much One cared. There was a goal yet to push for. To be sure, in the past, the goals had slipped mysteriously away, even as I was about to touch them, and the heart had been often sore; but I had learned—how strangely forgotten!—that though the goals of life are many, they are all in the same race, reaching toward the fulness of the stature of him they call Jesus the Christ. The goals midway are but to cheer. We run more easily for seeing a distance-mark near at hand. What matters it though the goal slips away even before our eyes? The race is no longer. We have merely lost the help of cheer by the way. We may even rejoice more heartily that we shall win uncheered.

My courage came back. I even thought with pleasure of the concert with which Mada-wanipee was to be favored that evening. The orchestra, which came from the city, was famous. The programme, too, was admirably suited to my mood.

The concert began with the glorious Fifth Symphony of Beethoven. As I listened, eyes closed, I fancied that I saw at the other end of the row a familiar face, — a face that has been before my eyes in memory for many years. I lived over again one evening in my student-life in Berlin.

It was a stormy night, that night in Berlin; but the company was light-hearted. At the other end of the row sat "My Glorious One," as I called her to myself, and so I was light-hearted, too. All day I had feared that she was ill, for she had been absent from a morning company in which I had expected to see her; but at the door we had just had a word together, and she had made me happy by treating as sincere the earnestness of my inquiry whether she had been ill. The first movement of the symphony carried me out of myself into another world. Yet, in the second movement, it was hard to live in any world at all, — the pleasure of living was almost a pain. I wanted to cry out for just a little less of the exquisite thrill which was running through me. It was doubly rich because I knew that Agnes was hearing and feeling it all. At the end of the movement I turned my head and opened my eyes. Her eyes were still closed; but the face, which was set off by the spotlessness of a white opera cloak and a crown of rich waving hair, was radiant. As I watched, she lifted her head, and her eyes fell upon me. She gave me a quick smile of sympathy. Once more, at the end of the concert, the same look was given me; and then I hurried away by dark, unfrequented ways, lest I should see some unsightly thing. I even grudged the streets entry to my eyes. I wanted to get away to the bridge, where I might look up into the sky and let that smile imprint itself upon my memory. I felt it slipping from me before I could fix it firmly. Oh, poor, weak imagination! The vision was at best but intermittent. I went home disconsolate. I had failed to make the vision mine, and she might never smile upon me so again!

How many times I had thought of that evening in Berlin! ' Even here in Madawanipee, years after, I could see and feel it all again. At the end of the second movement of the symphony, I opened my eyes, expecting to see the monotonous array of semi-animated Madawanipee Sunday-best. The majority of such audiences are stoical, — or are they even brutally inappreciative? Yet this was not what I saw. Was I still dreaming? Was not that the same face, the hair, the brow, the closed eyes, the coloring, the lips, the chin? While I was gazing, startled, the young woman opened her eyes; they were blue like the sea. Then I knew that I was not dreaming. Yet, in another moment, it was hard to be assured. Her face lighted with a smile that was quick, free, sympathetic. At the same moment, as she turned to speak, I heard tones that seemed to have come unbidden from my quickened memory. The tap of the conductor's baton reassured me that I was not dreaming.

It was thirty-five years ago that I had parted from "My Glorious One." It then seemed

44

incredible that God should have shown to me so much of earth's nobility if I were to be robbed of it forever. So in faith and hope and memory she lived with me for twenty years, and then she died.

Now perhaps my faith was justified. Was not this the same soul returned to earth in almost the same garb? If it had come back to earth, could it come back to me? Would it know me? Would it scorn my years? From the orchestra, which had gòne on to the Liebestod from Wagner's "Tristan und Isolde," seemed to come my answer. Even death cannot separate those who cling to each other. But I had no reason to think that Agnes cared even to remember me, — or had ever cared. Perhaps the likeness of my old love had come back to taunt me!

I looked into the girl's face again, and the fear fled. There could be nothing but cheer in those eyes and those lips and that brow. I had a curious feeling that they brought cheer in special measure for me. At the same time the orchestra took up a triumphal march, serious in

45

tone and rich in harmony. When we came out upon the sidewalk, the spell had not been wholly broken. I was living half in the past, half in the present. I must hear that voice once more. The young woman was but a little way ahead of me, and by dint of hurrying through the crowd I secured a place directly behind her. She was talking about the concert, but I seemed to hear a different story, — an old story, as old as the world, as old to me almost as my manhood. I was tempted to follow the voice as far as I could, but I refrained. Instead, after her party turned into a cross street, I hurried home, lighted a candle in front of an old daguerreotype upon my mantel, pulled my easy-chair before the open fire, and gave myself up to dreaming.

An hour later, my nephew tapped at my door. I did not let him in. Was it jealousy of youth that stayed my hand upon the latch?

IV.

SUNDAY was raw and sunless. There was not even a breeze to give something of life, — something to struggle against, and call out energy. Great masses of leaden clouds were lying heavily in the east. Now and then the faint outline of the sun could be perceived through the thinner clouds in the south, but it never gave even a promise of sunshine. The west was a monotonous gray. The atmosphere seemed to press upon one from all sides, and to penetrate every garment until it bore with all its rawness on one's very flesh. The light snow which had fallen early in the week had been but partially carried off by the daily thaws, and yet it had been but half frozen by night; it was lying in patches, smutty, soft, characterless. Even the church bells were oppressed by the day ; their vibrations fell heavy on the unbuoyant air. When I stepped out of the house on my way to church, I thought half the population of Madawanipee must be widowed. Three-fourths of the women were in black. Even the people who were supposed to be gay seemed to shrink within their clothes to get away from the harsh air.

A couple of my chance acquaintances happened to be passing. I fell into the line of church-goers behind them, and overheard their conversation.

" On such a morning," said one, " you forget that there ever was any sun, either for light or for warmth. You find it hard to be thankful for anything."

" Very true ; and it's hard to be hopeful for the future. We fear that when January 1 comes round, the balance will be on the wrong side of the balance-sheet. It's lucky the feeling goes off when the sun comes out."

" Yes ; I feel the change coming already. Look over there." As he spoke, he jerked his head to indicate the other side of the street.

A little girl, about three years old, wrapped in white, was approaching us. Every moment or two she looked back over her shoulder, as she trotted laughingly along, half running, half walking. A boy of five or six was pretending to chase her. Their cheeks were red, and their eyes were sparkling. The girl was chuckling with delight. Behind came a young woman, who encouraged the child by an occasional wave of the hand. When the little one had been caught, both children returned to her. The group was indeed a bit of sunshine. The young woman in the centre walked with light, well-poised step; the chubby little tottering figure on her right was looking up into her face, while the tongue told its broken story; on the left, and in advance, the boy was half walking, half hopping, now sideways, now backwards, trying, yet with patience, to get a chance to give his version of the story. One could not look at the six bright eyes and six red cheeks and call the day cold and dreary.

As they passed, I saw that the young woman was the one whom I had seen at the concert. The men in front of me were still watching.

"That's what it is to be young," said one of them.

49

"No, my friend," I interrupted, "that's not what it is to be young. Look at those young people ahead of you, — dull of face, half-crouching with fear of cold, listless in step. What you see across the street, in the young woman, at least, is not youth of years, but youth of heart."

There is one thing in an old bachelor's life that even the gayest youth may envy: he is utterly independent, — unless, indeed, he has allowed himself to get into ruts which have no cross-cuts. I come and go as the whim takes me; or does it better become my dignity to say that I come and go as my reason dictates? I change my dinner hour from six to seven, and yet I need not hurry to meet evening engagements. I forget to go to the post-office for two or three days, and it does n't matter. I go to bed at ten, or at two, or not at all, as I take a notion, and nobody protests, — unless my own nerves and digestive apparatus must be recognized as somebody. I am too lazy to get a new suit of clothes when the season changes, and the same laziness continues season after sea-

son, and yet nobody looks askance. I may go
to a strange church several weeks in succession,
and yet our little Madawanipee world does not
wonder what sudden "attraction" I have
found.

So when the group which I had been watching turned toward the Baptist church, I immediately changed my own intention, and followed.
I was curious to see more of the young woman.
Besides, I should have an opportunity to see
something of one of the interesting girls who
had grown up before my eyes. Miss Campbell
was just behind the others. Harry, my nephew,
was with her. She looked as if she were shivering with the cold. For once she was not
stately. She turned her head as I approached.

"Good-morning, Mr. Robertson. Are n't
we all very pious this morning?"

"We appear so outwardly. I can't speak
for our conditions within."

"If we are as humble inwardly as we look
outwardly, we must be in very humble frames
of mind," said Harry. "I have just been
telling Miss Campbell that she looks as if she

51

did n't dare say her soul 's her own this morning. This weather does n't agree with her."

"But if I freeze to death," Miss Campbell answered, with a triumphant smile, "my soul departs this life, and then it is n't my own any longer. Besides, would n't it be a bit blasphemous to go to church declaring that one's soul is one's own? It seems to me that I hear nothing else in church but that my soul is n't my own."

"In other words, you listen to only about one sermon in ten," suggested Harry.

"I 'm not going to talk to you any more," she exclaimed, with a pout. "You are not in the proper mood for church-going. I 'm going to talk to Mr. Robertson."

"What is the proper mood for church-going?" persisted Harry.

"Oh, a spirit of reverence and adoration and saying your prayers, and all that sort of thing."

"That 's just my mood. Have n't you seen adoration in my eyes every time you 've looked into them this morning, and have n't I been making sundry petitions?"

She could not repress the smile that came unwelcomed, but she did not look at him.

"Mr. Robertson," she said, "your nephew has been trying to persuade me that I ought to join the party which is going down to Hampton to-morrow to see the opening of the new academy. Don't you agree —"

"Pardon me," Harry broke in; "but I don't try to *persuade* people. I was trying to *prove* to you that you ought to go."

She looked at him, and laughed archly.

"I was n't talking to you," she said.

"But you were talking about me."

"You ought not to object to that," I suggested.

"But she was maligning me."

"How?" she asked.

"You said I persuaded. That's a woman's way; men prove, not persuade."

She looked him over with feigned new interest.

"In other words, you are neither man nor woman," she said; "for by your own confession you don't persuade, and most certainly you did n't prove."

53

We were now at the church door. I did not hear the rest of the mock controversy between them.

So far as the service was concerned, our selection of churches was poorly made. The preacher may have been a very worthy man, but his worth did not lie in his choice of messages for the congregation. He spent his half-hour in trying to reconcile us to the existence of poverty on the ground that the Bible sanctions it, — that is, recognizes it.

Most of the people soon decided that it was not worth while to listen to so childish a philosophy. Every one was in quest of some occupation. Even the children realized that less repression than usual was to be exercised against them. The little three-year-old whom I had watched on the street soon learned that if she could content herself with communication by means of eyes and smiles she need not lack for playmates. Her face was a marvel of mobility. The tiny mouth had scores of silent stories to tell; with the aid of eyes and nose, it had, perhaps, hundreds.

At first, though but two pews separated us, she did not think of counting me as one of her playmates. As she kneeled in her seat and surveyed the audience behind, her sweet, dimpled face was too charming to be looked at coldly. I smiled by myself as I watched her. She caught the smile, and thought that it was meant for her; but she did not return it. In a moment she looked back archly to see whether I was watching her. I scowled slightly, and she turned away with a puzzled expression. When she looked at me again, I pretended that I did not see her; but by directing my line of vision just above her head I could still catch the expression of her face. She was a trifle piqued. Could so young a girl be a thorough coquette? Did the perplexed look on her face mean that she was puzzling out how to get my attention again? I did not keep her long waiting; I feared to lose so charming a flirtation. I dropped my eyes to a level with hers. She turned her head slowly away, but kept her eyes on mine until the angle became uncomfortable; then the little chin went down behind the pew-back, the nose disappeared, and soon I could see only the hat and eyebrows. In another moment I saw two bright eyes. A bewitching, half-suppressed little smile made its appearance over the pew. It was too much for my gravity; I smiled outright, half in answer, half in amusement. Her smile could be no longer suppressed. I had won her little heart.

Yet, true to her woman nature, she was conscience-stricken at her confession. She clambered back to her place, and gave her attention to the people in front of her. I could see, however, that the fruits behind were still very tempting, for she half turned several times. I could watch the course of gradual surrender. It was surely not wrong to face the back of the church! So she resumed her kneeling position. Eyes, mouth, and tiny turned-up nose — for in mobile faces even noses can talk — held a long conference on the relative advantages of obeying conscience and of flirting with a stranger. The mouth insisted on flirting; the eyes inclined to it now and then, though they occasionally repented long enough at a time to put on a very serious air ; but the nose, in spite of a tendency toward jollity, was uncompromising in its adherence to the strictly legitimate. The conversation ran somewhat like this : —

" I wonder whether he is looking at me. I believe he is, and I 'm glad; but I must n't let him know it. — Of course he does n't expect me to smile at him. — I believe he does ; but I won't smile at a stranger. I wonder why he wants me to. — How pleasant he looks ! It makes me want to smile. — Oh, dear, it 's coming, and I can't help it ! — But I must n't. — There, I did n't ; but he ought not to look at me so steadily. — Now what is he laughing at ? I want very much to know. I shall have to smile, too, if he does n't stop. — Here it is ! and what a nice smile he gave me ! — Was n't it nice ? Let 's try again ! — There ! What fun ! — But perhaps it 's naughty. I think I 'll turn round."

By this time, her little brother had become solicitous for her moral welfare. The difference in age was just enough to give him almost a paternal interest in the tiny bit of mortality at his side. He spoke to the young woman. She smiled into the baby's face, and cuddled it close to her side.

At the close of the service, I heard her rich contralto voice ringing out in the grand old " Dennis."

I walked down the aisle with Mrs. Pembroke, the leader in the social life of Madawanipee and the prime mover in most of our charitable enterprises; for in our quiet town the two positions are not at all incompatible. In the vestibule we paused to complete our arrangements for a meeting of the associated charities.

"Pardon me a moment," she exclaimed suddenly, as she started forward.

"Ruth, I am delighted to see you. I heard that you had come, but I have n't caught a glimpse of you before." I turned, and found her talking to the stranger in whom I had become so much interested. "What a fortunate woman Mrs. Loring is!"

"I'm sure I'm glad to be with her, and to visit Madawanipee again. It does n't seem to change much."

"No, but we want to bring about a few changes. Mr. Robertson and I were just talking about one of them. Perhaps out of your experience in Boston you can help us. Let me introduce Mr. Robertson, if you have n't met him."

And so, suddenly, what had seemed hardly more real than a vision or a dream of the past became a concrete reality, which I could bow to, and even speak to by so commonplace a name as "Miss Appleton."

V.

FEW of the smaller New England cities afford material for greater variety of experience than Madawanipee. The heart of the city is alive with brisk commerce. The residence portion is divided so distinctly that it is literally true that one half does not know how the other half lives, — indeed, does not know the English-French that the other half speaks. This latter half lives on the plain below the mills. Its streets and door-yards are devoid of green, or other rest for the eye. Everything centres about the mills, and has the unmistakable factory air. The very people have been converted, to a certain extent, into machines. They take even their pleasures in a machine-like way, as if all were on the prospectus, and must be taken in due season. Perhaps their chief characteristic is that common to most factory populations, — their lives lack the contemplative element; in their eyes everything is not only objective, but practically devoid of relationships.

At the other end of the city, life is taken in different fashion, — at least, so it seems to the livers. Every house has its lawn, small though it may be, and grassy, shady sidewalks invite to cool saunterings. Many of the houses are old, and here and there one lifts its massive pillars to the eaves and reminds of the days when the men of the region lived to get the meaning out of life, and not merely to acquire. The electric cars have made their ravages, and the railroad takes and leaves travellers by its score of trains a day; but these serve only to extend a little of the bustle of the business world into the quiet streets where the townsman never takes it.

The city lies in the valley of a river large enough to give a sense of great power, and yet not too large for picturesqueness. Into this river flows the Madawa, — deep, silent, winding, fringed to the water's edge with low-hanging trees, and narrow enough for most satisfactory canoeing. It was locally known as "the stream." The town is built on the peninsula formed by the two rivers. It lies at the centre of a large farming district; and for the accommodation of the farmers, roads run into it from all directions, like spokes of a wheel converging at the hub. These are connected by cross-roads at various intervals, and thus by keeping on one of the peripheries of the wheel, as it were, one can take a walk of respectable length without getting far from town; or, if one wills, one can plunge straight into the country by a few minutes' walk from the post-office. My favorite walk, both for summer and winter, was to follow up the larger river as far as time would allow, then to strike across country to the Madawa, and finally to follow that down to town. I found almost as much enjoyment in winter as in summer. The flowers and birds were gone; but the snow, the winter winds, and the solitude were fruit for new sensations. I scandalized many of the prim ones among the townspeople by spending much of my leisure in summer in my canoe, and in winter on snow-shoes. In their minds, everything but walking and riding was beyond the pale of dignified procedure for a man of my years; but the obligation of being dignified I never more than half recognized, especially when one's vocabulary so abuses the word.

Thus it happened that, out of the mere love of sport, I was out one bitter morning in January to encounter the power of the winds. I was surprised, as I crossed the last field to the Madawa, to see before me, on the bank of the stream, a girlish figure braced against the gusts. As I approached, I saw that it was Miss Appleton. The crust was hard, and she walked as easily as upon a floor. Now and then she stooped to pick up a bit of snow-crust that her foot had broken, and threw it at some tree or out upon the ice. Sometimes when a fierce gust was blowing, she threw back the hood which protected her face, shook her head, and let the wind blow through her hair. If a tree stood in her path on the steep bank, she swung herself around it as easily as boys swing around a lamp-post. Her step was so light and springing that the crust seemed rather a guide than a support. Every motion, whether of head or arm or foot,

63

was but the escape of pent-up vitality. Of effort, there was none. She revelled in the closeness of her touch with Nature,—the white fields, the silent stream, the trees she brushed against, the wanton wind.

I came upon her just as she had thrown back her hood. Before I had time to say good-morning, she had replaced it.

"Isn't this glorious?" she exclaimed.

"Indeed it is. Every bit of the morning is every bit glorious."

"What a pity that people don't come out on such a day! Everybody stays at home by the fire and nurses her—and his—ability to take cold."

"Do you know that you have solved a problem for me? I have wondered all my life why most people take cold so easily. Their ability in that direction is almost unlimited. You have hit the explanation,—they nurse it."

"One might say more than that: they not only nurse, but nourish it. I cannot understand them. It is so joyous to be out in a cold gale, when the wind blows through one's clothing until even one's flesh is cold to the touch, and at the same time one feels the blood coursing through the arteries from the vigor of exercise. It's exhilarating, like keeping a wild beast at bay, and crying out to it, 'I may feel your teeth and you may scratch, but you can't bite; your power is only skin-deep.'"

As she finished speaking, we reached a place where the bank was not very steep.

"Don't be alarmed," she cried, gayly.

She took a few quick steps and a light spring, and before I could tell what she was about to do, she was sliding down over the hard crust toward the ice. I expected to see a fall; but when I saw her figure sway and bend gently to the one side or the other, accommodating its balance to the curves of the surface, I saw that I was watching no novice. A canoe never ran a rapid more gracefully. I was tempted to follow her; but it would have been unwise to trust my brittle bones in attempts to follow so lively a leader. She was back at my side almost as soon as I had made up my mind not to follow.

"Why did't you come, too?" she asked.

"Purely a matter of principle, I assure you," I answered, laughing; "I do not like to set a bad precedent. I know that some of your elders — it makes no difference who — could n't wisely follow you in such pleasures; I don't wish to set them the bad example."

"Which is equivalent to saying that I set the community a bad example."

As she spoke, she looked up into my face. Her eyes were deep and tender, and her lips were at the same time firm and mobile. The brown hood which she wore was a frame, in rich harmony, about her face. She seemed to come from another world.

"Ah, my dear Miss Appleton, you have heard of angels descending and ascending between heaven and earth. Would it be wise for me to follow one of them? Even if I could follow, would it be wise for me to set the precedent for my friends? Yet, even if I did, could the angels be blamed for the bad precedent?"

"Oh, what a pretty analogy! I am glad you did n't follow me, for then I should have missed all this."

The wind blew afresh, tipped back her hood a couple of inches, and let astray a few locks of brown hair about her temples. She was smiling in pleasure at my compliment. I forgot all about angels, — she was so much better than angels. A stray lock or two of hair and a touch of vanity are so gloriously human!

"Since you are so fond of Nature, I suppose you are not a city girl."

"Yes, and no. I was born in a large city, and I have lived there much of my time; but I have lived in small places so much that I have been able to get out into the country like this pretty often. Are you, too, fond of wandering about in the cold?"

"It's my great delight in winter; in summer I do the next best thing, wander about in the heat."

"How I wish I could go about as men can! It makes me angry to see them wasting their privileges. Look at the men at the fashionable summer resorts. Think of the powers of an able-bodied man, — to paddle, row, sail, ride, tramp, climb mountains, explore the wilderness,

everything that is inspiring in the way of sport,—
and then see him spotless in stiff linen and carefully brushed clothes, with button-hole bouquet,
sitting lazily in a carriage while another man
drives him around; then see him at afternoon
teas, talking small talk with a lot of girls as silly
as he.

> ' Oh, it was pitiful,
> Near a whole city full '

of that sort of thing!" She ended with a little
laugh, as if it would not do to seem to mean
seriously all she had said. She seemed half in
earnest, half in jest.

"If you talk that way much more, I shall be
inclined to call you a pessimist where society is
concerned."

"Oh, no!"

What a world of individuality there is in mere
accent! It was thirty years and more since I
had heard those two common monosyllables
spoken with quite that accent. It would be a
pleasure to hear her talk even without the deli-
cious quality of her tones, and even though she
had nothing new to say; her accent double-

freighted her words. It told of rare readiness of sympathy. One could not hear her and doubt that she was sincere, or even wonder whether her mind were wandering. Her every syllable had individuality; it was a living messenger direct from her mind and heart to another's. One was tempted to rest, as it were, on one's oars. It seemed almost needless when with her to try to be entertaining, or even to be clear; one felt not only as if she knew what one wished to say, but as if she were as much interested as one's self.

"I think winter is long enough for society, that is all," she said. "Perhaps other people can see what Nature has to show, and can hear what she has to say when many are about, but I can't; two or three are enough to make the enjoyment best, and they must be just the right ones. I want always to get the vision so clear that it will stay by me. I want it so that I can feel it all over again when I see it on canvas or in print. When we only half see Nature, we lose, not only while we are looking, but also for all moments of possible appreciation at second hand, either in memory or in pictures. In the city, during some of the winter, I live over again, in the art galleries, the days in the country. One can't dream over a beautiful picture unless one has made Nature one's own; and I can't do that within sight of many people and equipages, or within sound of many voices."

"You are clearly one of Nature's children. I saw that this morning before you saw me."

"Why, what was I doing?"

"Only throwing snow at the trees and swinging yourself around them in a very natural way, and letting the wind blow through your hair as if you and it were old playmates."

"The wind and I are old playmates, on water as well as on land.

"Ah, there you are!" she sang out suddenly.

We were approaching the gate of one of the outlying houses of the village. Miss Campbell was coming down the walk.

"Miss Campbell started out with me," she explained; "but she had an errand here, and went in to wait until I came back."

"Yes; and can you guess, Mr. Robertson,

what the errand was?" asked Miss Campbell, as she joined us, and we all started toward the village.

"Indeed, no! It is more than I can do to guess what a woman has in mind when I am looking at her. What shall I say when I hadn't even seen her for a week?"

"I thought you so good a judge of character that, when the circumstances were given, you could predict the actions of people you know."

"I am at a loss to understand any one's deserting Miss Appleton, — or," I added, in clumsy haste, "Miss Appleton's deserting you."

"I shall be jealous if you go on talking that way. You wondered that any one could desert Miss Appleton, and that so kind a girl as she should desert me. You are as bad as your nephew. You like to pay compliments that cut the wrong way."

She looked up in a playful way that I had become accustomed to, rather liked, in fact; but this time it was not altogether pleasing, — she had come too near the truth.

"You remind me sometimes," she continued, "of a teacher we once had at school. His name was Benjamin Fish,—'Beneficial' we called him. He was a thoroughly kind man at heart, but he was very sensitive. He felt personally slighted when we neglected our work. I suppose that is what made him so merciless, under the guise of civility, to the scholars who were careless. You must n't take too much of this as like yourself. One of the boys put together, in a perfunctory way, a number of chemical substances ready for an experiment. He did n't want to perform the experiment just then, so he put the retort aside, and then went to 'Beneficial' and asked him what to mark it.

"'How much hydrochloric acid did you say you put in?' asked Mr. Fish.

"'About a teaspoonful.'

"With even more dignity than usual, and in even deeper tones, Mr. Fish answered, without comment, 'Mark it "slops."' The boy never forgave him. Another boy once asked him how long he should hold a certain crazy concoction over the Bunsen burner to boil, and was told, very soberly, to 'boil it a week.' You are n't quite so bad as that; but there are often two sides to your speeches, as when you talk of Miss Appleton's deserting me."

"But you see it was n't a question of desertion at all," said Miss Appleton; "it was merely divided duty, and we both fought our own battles."

"And our weapons differed," added Miss Campbell. "We started out to fight the cold together. Ruth spurred me on by graphic descriptions of the fun of a fight with a cold, blowy morning on the river-bank. When we got here, I discovered that I had n't any weapons to fight with, and so I had to go into that house after some. Ruth must have had hers hidden somewhere, or else she has some strange way of fighting."

"But you did n't come back with your weapons, after all," laughed Miss Appleton.

"No. You see I found my chief weapon hardly portable, and it might burn my fingers. Besides, it smoked. I don't like *things* that smoke."

"Then you really deserted, I am afraid," I suggested.

"Oh, no! I merely stayed behind the breastworks, and used heavy artillery. Ruth was the light-armed infantry. I think she is rather grateful, too, that you came up as a reinforcement."

"Miss Appleton did not seem at all in need of reinforcement when I came up. I saw her before she saw me, and I had no notion that she had an enemy within range. She was contemplating the field with much apparent enjoyment and ease."

"Well," Miss Campbell responded, with a mock injured look, "the enemy wasn't after her, they were after me; she could afford to wander about light-armed. It needed a whole battery to protect me, for I was the real point of attack. Somehow I always need a lot of protection from this particular enemy. The weapons I like best are a good high-backed sleigh, plenty of robes, a very, very speedy horse, a young man who knows just how to hold the reins,—and that's all he will need to do to them if he knows how to drive,—and a piping hot supper at the other end of the road. I don't like to walk. Feet were made not to travel on, but to—to—just to vibrate on. Is n't that what a woman's for,—to vibrate? I mean is n't that what people expect of her?" She paused a moment. "She's to scintillate, and please everybody by being everything in general and nothing in particular, and never to take any initiative, but only to vibrate when her chords, and all that sort of thing, are touched."

"I suppose if that's all woman does, man does all the rest," suggested Miss Appleton.

"Oh, yes. He's the one that makes the 'wheels go round.' We're the ones who stand by and cry to 'shee wheels go wound.' If we can't see them, even at the risk of spoiling them, we cry. Did you ever think of it before? We make man's life miserable unless we are happy. To keep us happy, he makes the wheels go round; but then we meddle, and spoil it all. Is it strange that the world is a strange place?"

"After all, is n't it the men themselves who see the wheels go round?" I asked.

"Yes, perhaps it is, — at least, some kinds of wheels. They won't let us see them go round. We have to content ourselves with hearing about them."

"In other words, you only hear the watch tick."

"Perhaps that's why women are so much afraid of getting old," said Miss Appleton. "They know only the monotonous tick, and don't see any of the motion that makes it. They get to think of time as a thing which takes away, but never gives."

"My small brother," suggested Miss Campbell, doubtfully, "would correct you there, and say that, though Time never gives, he 'gives away,' — that he's a horrible fellow for 'giving away.' He would just delight to get a chance to say so to some of the young old maids in town."

"What is an old maid?" I asked.

"An old maid," answered Miss Campbell, readily, "is one who is old enough to know better."

"Is that why the limit of age varies so much?"

"Certainly. Some don't know enough to marry until they are thirty, and yet we don't call them old maids; others are old maids at twenty-five. They know better; but they are too stupid, or too lazy, or something, to catch 'the good fish in the sea.'"

"You forget that they need bait," suggested Miss Appleton, "just as you forgot your own weapons this morning."

"Oh, no! Why, flies are better than live bait, I'm told; and a woman who can't make her own flies, and hooks, too, for that matter, does n't deserve to catch fish. I'll risk a bright woman, even if she has to make every bit of her own tackle."

"If that's the feminine point of view," said I, "it's time the men were suspicious as well as suspected. The bulk of our literature, and especially of our dramatic literature, puts suspicion upon the men. It becomes interesting to hear that women not only angle for men, but angle for them with flies."

"Why, deception is the great civilizer," declared Miss Campbell. "To get rid of our

77

delusions is all we live for. So if we did n't have any delusions, life would n't be worth living."

" What 's the particular delusion you live to get rid of?" asked Miss Appleton.

" That I 'm not so good as I ought to be."

"I suppose, then," said I, "that it 's not allowable to ask you whether life is worth living."

" Oh, yes," she laughed, " and I ought to be a good authority,— I find it so. I doubt whether I ever accomplish the end, you know. It 's rather hard to persuade one's self that one is as good as one ought to be, — as hard as it is to persuade one's self that one is as warm as one ought to be on a day like this. But I 'm going to be as warm as I ought to be in a few moments. Won't you both come in and have some hot chocolate ? "

We reached her home as she spoke. Miss Appleton accepted the invitation, but I kept on my way. The thought that I had learned some of Miss Appleton's favorite walks was cheer enough for me.

78

VI.

HOW dear a town becomes if one is always
on the alert to catch sight of a particular
face! Heretofore I had felt like a sojourner in
Madawanipee; it seemed suddenly to have become a part of my life. Every morning when
I left the house, I scanned the street to see
whether Miss Appleton chanced to be in sight.
I never passed a cross-street without looking up
and down for her. It would be so easy to miss
seeing her sometime that I took every precau-
tion. I chanced upon her just often enough to
keep the hope from dying.

One morning, as I came down the steps, she
was a little way ahead of me. I soon overtook
her.

"Is it legitimate to be so late in starting out
for the day?" she asked, with a smile. "I think
I heard a door close just before you appeared."

"Are n't all things legitimate when their
complements are not wanting?"

79

"What virtue can make up for a late beginning of the day?"

"A late ending, to be sure."

"But one must know why the day ended late before one can justify such an excuse. You see I am not lenient to people whose ways are a little off color."

"I see. I pity one whose sins should fall under your eye. Would you condone my late appearance if I should prove that I was engaged in a laudable enterprise last night?"

"What a hard judge you make me out to be! I must search with double diligence for the beam in my own eye. I hope you will tell me about your laudable enterprise, so as to put me to shame; for I was n't a bit laudable last night. I treated an estimable young man very unkindly, though I must say that it was done unconsciously."

"There, now I have my retaliation; for my laudable enterprise was doing just what you failed to do. I treated an estimable young man with the utmost kindness. I have a nephew in town. He was in a proper mood for listening to a good lecture last night. I gave it to him."

"Do you call that kindness?"

"Did n't you ever lecture a young man and call it kindness?"

"Perhaps,—in fun."

"Oh, no, in earnest! Of course you have. Something has got hold of this nephew of mine. I could imagine that he had fallen in love, or was getting within sight of the precipice over which to fall, if I did n't think the girl who put him in danger was not here. He seemed to be bewitched a few weeks ago; but he told me afterward that the girl, a stranger in town, had gone away. I know that he was not so badly smitten that she could disturb his equanimity after she had gone. He talked of her for days, though he had never met her. He does n't work, nor play, nor do anything else. His work is n't pressing him hard, and so he neglects it. He chiefly dreams. Last night he dropped in to see me about eleven, dreamier than ever, and I tried to wake him up; but I fear he went off to dreaming again before he got home."

81

"Is dreaming hard to cure?"

"Easier than the leprosy, only. There is one cure, or rather one physician, for every dreamer; but often that is the very one impossible to employ."

"I hope you succeeded in cheering your nephew up. That is," she added hastily, "I hope you are the physician for him."

"Oh, I did n't say that he was blue. I suspect, on the other hand, that I but confirmed him in his bad habit."

I noticed that she was a trifle embarrassed when I corrected her and said that he was not blue; and I thought it strange that she should care so much about so slight a matter.

"I must turn down this street," she said, as we reached the next corner. "I hope — but won't you come, too? Perhaps you have n't been there. I 'm going to the jail to see a man convicted of stealing from a cousin of mine. He seems to like to see me, and I have been there a good many times. It is very interesting; so many curious types! And being there for the purpose of seeing a special one, I can look about

82

and see the others when they are not on exhibition, as it were, to curiosity-seekers. They are very different, then. Many seem to resent being shown as curiosities, and they put on hard, defiant faces; whereas alone they show something of natural feeling. Will you come?"

"Thank you, gladly."

We were ushered into a long corridor from which the cells opened. The special subject of Miss Appleton's visit was near the door. He was a rough, sensual-looking fellow, of thirty or thereabouts, with an eye that seemed to have degenerated into viciousness. He chanced to see me first. It seemed almost as if he could not be touched by anything noble or beautiful. Yet when he saw Miss Appleton behind me, his scowl vanished, his eyes sparkled with delight and gratitude like a child's. Even the sensuality of the face seemed to pale, and something of the buried nobler self shone through the marks of vice. He watched her eagerly, passionately; but the passion had none of the ruffian in it. It was the passion of a child for some adored man or woman.

"Good-morning," she said, with a smile, as she stopped before the door of his cell. "How is Mr. Murphy this morning?"

"Oh, I'm fine! as fine as any one can be without a free look at the sky and the sunshine; and I hope you are feeling as fine as an angel yourself, Miss Appleton."

"I'm always well, you know. I'm as well as any one can be who isn't an angel," she added, with a gay smile. "You see we all have some limitations. You might feel better if you were free to go about, and I might feel better if I were an angel. I'm not ready to be an angel yet, for I want to come here and see you a few times more first; and this time I want to introduce you to my friend, Mr. Robertson."

I ought to have been prepared for this; but singularly I had been so busy with thoughts about my companion that I had not thought of my own duties. I could not well tell the man that I was pleased to see him, for when at the jail it would be kinder to wish him elsewhere. I could not congratulate him on the beauty or coziness of his surroundings; I could not even congratulate him on having so faithful a friend as Miss Appleton, for that would but emphasize his need of such a friend. What a pity it is that our wits get slow with our limbs! By rare luck, just as I reached Miss Appleton's side, ready for the introduction, I found a ground of common interest with him.

"I am glad to see a man," I said, "who has managed to keep Miss Appleton for his friend as long as she tells me you have. I know more than one person who would count it an honor to possess her friendship at all."

He smiled faintly at first, as if bound by common civility to smile at anything I might say in the way of greeting; and then his heavy face lighted up slowly as he looked at her.

"I 've heard some of the ladies who come here say God is everybody's friend, and won't let us drive His friendship away. It ain't because we deserve it; perhaps it 's because we don't deserve it. That 's the way " — here he turned to me — " Miss Appleton 's made. It ain't nothin' to my credit that she 's my friend; it 's only her kindness."

"I see he doesn't understand," she said. "He doesn't see how I get any pleasure out of coming here. He doesn't know my hobby, or mania, of wanting other people to read the books I like. He doesn't tell you about the books I bring him, and make him read. I begin to think that if I'm not careful I shall make him hate the very sight of books. Yet he always seems to read what I bring, and he does it as patiently as any one could ask, — or, at least, he never shows anything but patience when I'm about."

I saw in his face the light which indicates that one is laboring to catch and bring out some elusive thought. I turned away for a moment, as if interested in something at the end of the corridor, and waited rather curiously. It was not long in coming. He spoke slowly, looking down.

"I never was given to showing impatience because my mother brought me anything extra good for a present; and since I was a child no one ever did anything for me until now."

He seemed doubtful of the issue of this experiment. Several moments passed before he looked up. He found Miss Appleton looking into his face with those wonderful eyes of hers, and that wonderful, sympathetic smile, — seeming to know all that was noble in him, rejoicing in it, and believing that it would prevail. He quickly brightened, like a child who finds praise where it feared blame.

I left them talking, and passed on through the corridor to see whether the other cells were occupied. I noticed a hard-looking man, perhaps beyond middle age, leaning with his face pressed closely against the bars and gazing toward Miss Appleton. I returned down the corridor; but on passing up a second time, I found that the man had not moved even his eyes. At the upper end I paused to get a view of him without his seeing me. He seemed straining his ears as well as his eyes. When I reached his cell on the return, I stopped.

"Do you happen to know the man with whom my friend is talking?" I asked.

"Yes, sir, very well."

"Is there anything particular about him, or is he like" — I was going to say "the rest of

you," but checked myself in time to turn it into
— "other people?"

"He ain't like other people, or he would n't
be here," was the simple reply. "But he ain't
like the other men here, — leastwise he ain't
now; he was as bad as any of 'em when he first
come."

"What has happened to him?"

"I don' know what you call it, but it's that
young lady what done it."

"How?"

"Oh, jus' comin' to see him, an' talkin' to
him like he was a man an' not another sort o'
critter. An' then she brings him books, — not
the kin' they call Sunday-school books, but books
about real people an' such like. It seems to kind
o' wake up his insides, — makes him think, yer
know, an' want to do better when he gets out.
She don't go preachin' to him, but jus' talks with
him the same as she would any feller."

"You think he likes to have her come and
bring books, then, do you?"

"Likes it! It takes the sap all out o' him
if she don't come jus' when he expec's her.

"Say," he continued confidentially, after a moment's pause, "s'pose she'd let me have one o' them books she let him have last week? He tol' me about it. He said it kind o' opened his eyes. If it's goin' to open a feller's eyes to the sort o' thing she sees, I'd kind o' like to have mine opened for a while, to see what it's like."

I gladly carried the message; and even more gladly, if possible, she answered it in person. It was hard for the man to repress sufficiently his delight at having her come to speak to him. I lingered a moment after she had returned to her special ward, and could see the new light in his face, the new energy even in his posture.

"I've watched her every time she's been here when we wasn't workin' in the workshop," he exclaimed enthusiastically; "an' I count up, just as the other feller does, an' guess when she's goin' to come again. I never seen a lady like her before. Lots o' women come here, an' a good many of 'em talk to us; but they ain't like her. She don't talk to that feller about his sins, an' ask him to be better. She jus' talks to him as she'd talk to any one confined in the house, an' tries to amuse him an' cheer him up. She don't have to talk about his sins, or ask him to be better. Her beautiful face an' her smile an' her voice, quiet but strong, like the brooks I used to know when I was a kid, do all that. She seems to believe in a feller, an' make him want to show her he can do what she wants him to."

I walked home with Miss Appleton.

"I don't suppose it would do any good for me to tell you what I think of your work there this morning," I said.

"Yes, it would do good, whatever you say. You can help me to find the right thing to do."

"No, I can't do that. Even if it was ever possible, I am too late now."

She looked up with an expression half of fear, half of pleasure, questioningly, until I continued:

"We do not search for things which were never lost, — certainly not for things which we have always had."

"If you are going to talk that way, you can't help me."

"So I feared. You are beyond help. Even praise will not help you. You are too independent, too courageous, to find help in anything of the kind."

"Please do not talk like that. Do you forget that I am a woman? At least," she continued, slowly, as if a new thought had interrupted her, "I hope I am not so hard, so self-confident, so emancipated," — she smiled a little here, — "as to be beyond the help of sympathy."

"Forgive me! The trouble is that my sympathy is so great. I saw so much of the good you have done those two men that I did not stop to think that you are only a woman still."

Her quick look of gratitude forgave me.

VII.

A S the winter passed on into spring, my heart seemed to grow young again, — young again, did I say? No, not that! I cannot admit that it ever grew old. But there is a change in the heart. We need not abandon hope of pleasure, — unless, indeed, our lives have been so squandered that we know chiefly the pleasures of the body, — we need not abandon the hope of rendering service; but one thing is lost forever, — the hope of winning some maiden's love. In that respect our lives have been lived, and we are as dead. How selfish we are! Because the hope of winning love has gone from us, we forget the power of loving; we close our hearts against the giving of that which, given, leaves us richer. Under the touch of this young girl's life I found my heart opening. I could not hope to touch her heart even so lightly as to quicken its beating; yet that was no reason why my own should not be quickened, strengthened, opened to the inspiration of noble womanhood.

Perhaps it was the old love with which I had lived alone so many years breaking from its bounds under her magic touch. My Agnes seemed come back to earth again, ignorant of me. I could no more help worshipping her now than when my blood was youthful. Years ago, after she had been lost to me, I had not the right even to try to serve her; now, in this new love, the right of service, at least, could not be denied me.

Doubtless I was rather childish about it, but I watched eagerly for any little want of hers which I could supply. It chanced that I overheard her say that she loved the little plant called the gold-thread, and longed for a glimpse of it. I had longed all spring for a note of the white-throated sparrow; and I knew that if she longed for the flower as I longed for the bird, it would be worth my while to make an excursion in quest of one. I had found the plant growing, a year or two before, in the woods near White Pond; and thither I betook myself at the first opportunity. The day was one of the perfect ones of spring, when Nature is full of her annual task, but working so peacefully that one hardly thinks of change. It was a delight merely to live. I was doubly repaid for my pains; for when I emerged upon the Prescott Road, I carried a large bunch of the plants.

Along the western side of the road the woods had been cut for fuel, and each year's cutting could be traced by the varying heights of the new growth. The woods were sprinkled with pine, and the red needles strewed the sloping ground. The first touch of spring had flushed the tops of the bare trees. As one looked from the road, a terraced bank of crimson-pink — the ground, the tops of bushes, of saplings, and of trees — rose from one's feet to the sky. The sun had set; and the east was illumined with the reflection, more peaceful even than the original, of the western pinks. It seemed to typify the love of my old age, the reflection of the love of my youth. Below the road the river had spread out to a pond, and from overhead it had caught the sunset colors, reflecting them once more. I was in the midst of one of Nature's color displays, — the red of the ground and the trees, the deep blue of the upper sky, the pink of the east, the doubly delicate pink of the crystal lake. The black shadows under the western shore gave the needed touch of intensity.

Everything was in perfect peace, — so beautiful as to be almost sad. When I reached the village, it was so dark that people could not be recognized except face to face. I intended to carry the flowers to Ruth in the evening; but in the hope that I might see some trace of her I slackened my pace before I reached the house where she was staying. From the yard I heard children's voices, and then a voice from the piazza.

"No-o," came the answer, in a piping little voice, out of the darkness, "I want to hear Wuth thing thum more."

Another voice, boyish, but as eager, took up the plea: "Miss Appleton is going to sing us the birdie song, and then we'll come in."

"Yes, Annie, we shall be in very soon. I promised them one little song. It's not at all cold out here."

How I loved the tones of that voice!

I saw approaching slowly up the garden path a tall figure in a light gown, and two small figures, — one pudgy, one slender. When I saw that they would not come very near me, I stopped to hear the song.

It was Soederberg's "A Birdling sang on the Linden-Bough." At the words, "In spring he'll surely be returning," the voice, though so quiet that it scarcely could have been heard from the middle of the street, was rich as with certainty and joy in the words.

My peace was gone. It was very foolish, but a dart of jealousy went through me. I knew that she could never love me, could never think of me with anything more than kindness, or perhaps admiration, — should I say veneration? Yet she was my all! I tried not to be selfish; and I told myself that if I knew the man who was to come, and knew him worthy of her, I should rejoice with her. But if he should be a mere stripling, unformed and untried! Perhaps I could even stand the stripling, and have faith in him because she had faith in him ; but if he were tried and found wanting in the noblest manhood! That would go hard with me. If she had been blinded; if her eyes had never been opened to know a man when she saw one ; if she had given her love to a man whose life had not been lived worthily of her, — my last dream of happiness was gone.

I wandered slowly home. Harry was at my desk, reading the morning's city papers. On the table stood a glass of water with a bunch of gold-thread. I stopped on the threshold, and we looked at each other.

" I wonder," laughed Harry, " whether you can tell me where I can find some growing gold-thread ? "

" You don't seem to need the information. Whose are these ? "

" I picked them."

" I did n't know that you ever brought home flowers."

" I don't commonly. I picked these for some one else."

My curiosity was excited. Ruth was the first person whom I had ever heard express a fondness for the flower; and it seemed strange that Harry should have brought them at just this time unless they were for her. I remembered, too, that he had been present when she had spoken of them.

"Who is the favored person?" I asked.

"Ruth Appleton."

I am afraid that I winced. Just why, it would be hard to say. Indeed, I have preferred not to ask myself just why. I suppose my fancy jumped clear of all reasonableness, and ran its own wanton way. Childish I suppose it was for me to be jealous when I heard her sing; but after once giving way, it was not strange that I looked with great suspicion upon Harry. I knew him unworthy of her, and yet I knew him better worthy of her than many a more promising youth.

"I suppose it is safe to guess," said Harry, "that your flowers are for Ruth, too."

"They are intended for Miss Appleton." I spoke in a corrective tone.

"That's what I said."

"I understood you to say 'Ruth.'"

"Yes; Ruth Appleton."

"I call her Miss Appleton when I speak of her."

There was little use in trying to correct Harry, and make him observe the delicacies of either speech or demeanor. He was a boy still, and a boy he will always remain. I was free to correct and scold him as often as I saw occasion, but my progress was not always encouraging. His mother had been my only sister; and at her death, Harry became my charge. Our relations were almost as close as those of father and son; but I had striven rather to give them the freedom and companionship, so far as the difference of age would allow, of brothers.

"If her name is Ruth, I might as well call her so," he said.

"Do you call her so before her face?"

"I have n't yet."

"You contemplate it?"

He shrugged his shoulders, thrust his hands deep into his pockets, and looked at the ceiling.

"I should n't be surprised," he said.

He spoke as a man might speak who contemplated astonishing his friends by buying a palatial yacht or a beautiful estate. It was well that I had not seated myself. I laid down my hat, and began to walk up and down the room. Of the varied emotions which stirred me, indignation was uppermost. If Ruth had promised to marry him, his tone betrayed his unworthiness; if she had not, it was nothing less than insolent.

He did not notice my agitation. I was glad that he felt talkative and was likely to explain himself before I needed to speak.

"I suppose you 'll give me your flowers to add to mine, since it 's all in the family," he laughed. "One big bunch makes a better showing than two little ones. We 'll call it a joint tribute to her beauty.

"She is a beauty, is n't she?" he went on. "The different elements seem to be put together just right in her to make the finest effect. At one time or another in my life, I have thought half a dozen girls just about right. Kitty Davener was a daisy, but she is n't so young-looking now.

I used to think nothing could be any finer. She used to be such a cute little thing — dimpling cheeks, babyish mouth, questioning eyes (as if she were afraid you were trying to 'bluff' her), snub nose — that a fellow wanted to cuddle her right inside his overcoat, and carry her home to help him fill his easy-chair.

" Then, as I speak, I can see the rhythm of Laura Campbell's lithe body, so luxuriously moulded. And then think of that wonderful complexion of hers, — so smooth, so fair, so soft! It makes a fellow want to get up against her cheek, just to get the sensation of mere lusciousness.

" But Ruth Appleton is n't like the others," he continued ; " she has n't quite the same effect on me. She 's doubtless quite as fine, and when I stop to think of it, I realize it ; but it is generally only unconsciously that one has the sense of how very fine an animal she is, with her tall, well-knit figure, clear, vigorous complexion, and vigorous carriage. She 's so fine an all-around girl, with her clear head and plucky spirit, that the other girls are n't in the same game with her.

She suits me to a T. It would n't be half bad if she had the same sort of feeling toward me."

"Then you have n't told her yet all the admiration she calls out?"

"No."

"But if you are in love with her," I asked, "what about Laura Campbell and the love you thought you had for her before you saw Miss Appleton?"

"Nothing new."

"What do you mean by that?"

"Our relations have n't changed."

"Then what do you call them?" I asked, in astonishment.

"Just now they come without calling; they are hanging fire, I guess."

"Well, what will they ever amount to?"

"I don't know. Miss Appleton knows more about it than I. If I can get her for myself, why, naturally, I shall lose Laura; if I lose Ruth, I hope to get Laura."

In spite of my fear lest I should alienate his confidence, I found it hard to keep my temper.

"Do you mean that you love both girls at once?"

"Not exactly that; but I have stopped loving Laura for a while, as it were, to see whether I can win Ruth."

"Be good enough to call her Miss Appleton until she grants you permission to speak of her as Ruth, please. What do you suppose she would think of such a proceeding, if she knew?"

"She ought to feel highly complimented that I should keep my affection for Laura waiting on herself."

"Pardon my bluntness, but you are very much mistaken; she would scorn you, if she knew it. Do you think she wants such a love as you could give her?"

"I would give her all I have. No one else would have any of it."

"Doubtless. Perhaps I ought to have asked what kind of love you could give her. I should like to hear her express an opinion of the love of a man who, because he could n't win the girl he would like to marry, would marry a girl because he could win her. You say that if you can't win your first choice, you will not hesitate to ask in marriage a girl whom you call in your heart your second choice. I hope the second choice would be satisfied with the love she got. I call that a bargain, not marriage."

"But I told you Miss Appleton was my first choice. I love her well enough to satisfy her, or any woman. I adore her. She just fits my notion of what a woman ought to be. I love just such blue eyes and brown hair and innocent nose and smiling lips and tall figure and musical voice and gracious temper."

"Ah, do you? If I were her lover, I should love blue eyes because hers are blue; I should love brown hair because hers is brown; I should love such lips and figure and voice because hers are such. See the difference?"

"Y-yes — what little there is."

"There 's all the difference in the world."

"At any rate, Miss Appleton is my first choice, and that 's what you say she cares about; so I am all right on that score."

"It is n't enough that she shall be first choice. Quality of love is just as important. She will never marry a man who *could* marry a woman second in his heart."

He sat in silence for a time.

" I 'm glad that I don't see things as you do," he said, at last. " Still," he continued, a moment later, " if your point of view is the correct one, I wish I could see from it."

" I fear that we shall never see from the same points of view. I have tried to show you mine. Let 's change the subject."

It was perhaps fortunate for my future peace of mind that after my conversation with Harry no peculiar opportunities either for aiding or hampering him in his suit chanced to fall in my way. In spite of my fondness for him, I could hardly have looked on quietly while a man who spoke as he spoke sought to make Ruth his wife.

I did not give him my flowers. When he had gone, I sent for a messenger. I wrote a few words on my card, and attached it to the bunch ; but before the messenger had closed the door, I called him back, and removed the card.

VIII.

I WAS not patriotic on Memorial Day. I somehow dislike a crowd, because it is a crowd. When I started out for my daily exercise, I took a direction away from the cemetery. I wandered across fields and through groves, regardless of the right of property in land. Ruth was in my thoughts, as usual. We were on the best of terms; for not a week passed without a forenoon or afternoon of walking or riding or canoeing together. She found no other girls who wanted so much exercise; I wanted no other companion : so we went together, — and quiet, unconventional Madawanipee did n't care. They say that we cannot have our cake and eat it too; yet I seemed to do so. I had the memory of Highbank days with Agnes, and yet with Ruth I was living them all over again. All, did I say ? No, not quite all ; I am an old man now.

I passed over a knoll, and came suddenly upon

a man's figure stretched prostrate on the grass, face downward. The arms were folded under the forehead. I did not wish to intrude if the position was voluntary, and yet I thought it wise to investigate. I stopped to watch for a moment. Just as I was about to go forward, the man turned over. I recognized him as a fellow-boarder, who had within the last three months come to Madawanipee from a hamlet forty miles away. He had but recently cast his first vote.

"Your position startled me," said I, when he recognized me. "I did n't know but that I had found a case for the coroner. Which would you rather that it would be, a murder or a suicide?"

As I spoke, I drew nearer, and saw that his face was drawn hard, as if almost in despair.

"I don't know as it would make much difference," he answered.

He sat up, and tried to throw off his mood; but my chance greeting had made it harder than ever.

"You really look as if you would n't mind either very much. What is the matter? Are you sick?"

"Oh, no, not at all." There was no life in his voice.

I had taken a fancy to him as soon as I saw him at the house. I wanted him to succeed in life, but his mood warranted the expectation of anything but success. I sat down on a rock near him, even at the risk of intruding; I meant at least to turn the current of his thoughts.

"A man has no right to look as you do unless something is the matter with him," said I, trying to smile. "A dozen such people in a community would hide the sun. You owe it to the world to cheer up."

He looked up at me almost fiercely, with the old, old question on his lips.

"How much do I owe the world? It's your devilish town here that has made me as I am. Do I owe the town a bright face in return? I came here with some faith in God and man, — and woman, too. They have pretty nearly taken it all away. Nobody cares for the good in him or in other people. Everybody lives on the brutish side of himself here; and, what makes me hate myself, I begin to wonder whether it was n't so at home, only I did n't see it because I was so green."

"I know how you feel. I 've been in the same place myself. You 're morbid. You have been looking at one side of life too long, — and the wrong side. You have shut yourself up in your shell, and have thought that you could see into other people's shells ; but you must remember that you can't, until you have opened your own so as to see out better. Take my word for it, for awhile, that your old faith in the good is all right, — not only as a faith, but as a working principle. You will see it for yourself, soon."

I succeeded in cheering him a bit ; but, best of all, I got a promise from him to go up stream with me on his part holiday, Saturday. I appreciated his desperate state. There is, perhaps, none harder in life, — alone, unloving, and unloved ; the evil thrusting themselves in one's face, the good holding back their skirts because one has not been " properly presented."

As soon as we parted, I made what I thought a bold move. I went straight to Ruth. When

I arrived, she was telling Harry, who was standing hat in hand, that she would be delighted to join a sailing party for Saturday afternoon. My hopes fell. I saw that I had saddled my young friend Cobb with myself for a companion on Saturday, and had lost the one help which I had meant to carry him. As soon as Harry left, I told her my errand, but said that I withdrew from the field.

When I had left the house, Miss Campbell came into my mind as a possible substitute. She was bright enough to entertain Cobb, but she had little of the deep sympathy which I wished to put in his way. At all events, she would make my little party more cheerful; and cheer I must have. I found her at home, and apparently glad to go.

The next afternoon, however, a note came from Ruth asking whether my invitation for Saturday still held good. I hurried to her in joyful surprise.

"Yes," she said; "I am regretting what I did yesterday. I may as well be frank with you. I was pleased that Mr. Templeman should ask me to go with him; besides, I wanted to be with the party. I knew I ought not to go with him, — it is n't necessary to say why, — but the temptation was too great. He seemed to care so much that my vanity was tickled, and I consented against my better judgment. It 's perhaps just as wrong to decline to go now as it was to accept in the beginning. There is bound to be wrong somewhere, for it 's already done. I would rather go with you. I may do harm by going to the sailing party on the river; but I can't do much harm by going up the stream with you and the young friend you want me to meet. So I 've asked Mr. Templeman to excuse me, and I 'm going with you, if you 'll take me."

"Indeed I shall. I was very much disappointed yesterday when I thought I could n't have you. Miss Campbell is going too, and we shall try to have a jolly little party."

"I am glad Miss Campbell is going; she is always so wide awake."

I told her nothing about young Cobb, except that he was from the country, — a long way off,

— was very lonesome, and was, I suspected, very bashful. We planned to take a luncheon up the stream with us, and stay until early evening, so as to get the best lights and shadows on the trees.

I went to Miss Campbell at once to tell her of the addition to the party. I innocently expected her to be as glad as I.

"Ruth Appleton will be just the girl for that sort of excursion," she commented. "If the young man is lonesome among strangers here, as you say, she will help greatly to cheer him up. She's such a homelike, domestic body." She had been looking into my face when she first spoke. As she continued, she looked down, and toyed with a card on the table. "Just to look at her makes one feel comfortable. She's almost grandmotherly, sometimes. Everyone falls in love with grandmothers, you know. Perhaps that's why every one falls in love with her. Every one does, from the driver of the town offal-wagon to the Baptist minister. A girl who doesn't seem grandmotherly doesn't count at all since she came."

There was a touch almost of bitterness in her tones ; yet she was smiling.

"It 's a new style, perhaps," she added. " New styles are generally taking — at first."

"Of course, then, you are glad to have so many chances for studying the new style ; I have seen you with Miss Appleton several times."

" Yes, I was with her a good deal when she first came ; but you see I caught the style at last, and don't need to study it any more."

" And now you are one of those who help to spread it ? "

" Oh, no ! It is n't catching like that. Nobody ever caught it from me. Besides, it 's not at all dangerous ; most of us get over it very easily."

I tried in vain to get at the meaning of this remark. It seemed to reflect a little unpleasantly upon Ruth, — unless, indeed, Miss Campbell had over-reached herself in trying to say something bright. Before I had made up my mind how to interpret it, she spoke again : —

" Now that Miss Appleton has consented to go, you don't need me. She can grandmother your friend, whereas I could n't even cousin him. You would n't miss me much if I did n't go, after all, would you?"

"Why, I have been counting on you, of course."

"Oh, that 'of course' tells it all. You know what we always mean when we say 'of course' about ourselves. It's only a little compromise with our consciences for telling a little less than the truth, — or is it sometimes a little more? You see you don't care much about my going now that you have Miss Appleton. I have an invitation to go to Richmond for a few days, starting to-morrow. If I am to go with you, I must give up Richmond."

"Indeed, I shall be sorry to miss you, but you would probably be as sorry to lose the visit. So I excuse you, if I must; but I am sorry to lose you."

"What a sorry affair we are! But it will soon be over. I 'll find comfort in Richmond, and you 'll find it in Miss Appleton — like Naomi."

I began to suspect that Miss Campbell was not altogether happy. Harry had been paying her much less attention in the last few weeks than formerly. This might or might not affect her frame of mind. If matters stood between them as was commonly reported, it should. Besides, an interruption had come in the series of excursions which she and I had taken with semi-regularity since my first interest in her as a young school-girl. She could not care much for this; but she might care for the cause of it. She would have come very near the truth if she had said that people deserted her for Miss Appleton. I had done so unconsciously. I suspected that Harry had done so, too, though he was probably thoroughly conscious of it. A girl of her disposition could not help caring that another had supplanted her, even though she cared but little intrinsically for the position lost. At all events, she was just then none too fond of Ruth.

When I called for Ruth, Saturday afternoon, she was putting up the lunch. She took me into the dining-room to help. I watched her deft fingers making small parcels and packing them into incomprehensibly small space.

"Did you say that he is very lonesome?" she asked, as she examined a flask carefully before putting in cold tea.

"I don't know whether he is always so, but he has been frightfully so during the last week."

"Is it homesickness?"

"Much of it is not; perhaps some of it is. He has unfortunately seen the worst side of life here, and he has begun to lose faith in the good; he begins to fear that all good appearances are but shams."

"How horrible!"

"I want to give him a glimpse of the best of—" I stopped. It might not be wise to tell Miss Appleton just what I thought of her. Besides, none of us is quite himself if he is supposed to be on his best behavior. If we know that others are watching us, and are expecting us to do certain acts of graciousness, we are uncomfortably self-conscious. Spontaneity is gone, or, at least, though it be not, we are never sure of it. So I spared her. "I want to get him away from the town and from all the thoughts connected with it," I said.

She was putting knives and forks into the basket. She stopped with them in mid-air.

"Is he very bashful, do you think?"

"I really don't know how he would be with a young woman; I fear so."

She put the knives and forks at the bottom. She hesitated a moment, and then took them out again.

"Wherefore?" I asked.

"You will see when the time comes," she answered gayly.

She started for the kitchen, but came back.

"Are you willing to be a martyr for this young man's sake?" she asked.

"How much of a martyr?"

"Oh, suppose you knew that your canoe would tip you out, would you still go for his sake?"

"Yes, provided you were there to rescue me with your strong swimming stroke. Why?"

"I was wondering how much you care to please him."

She went out. In a few minutes she returned with another flask. An ill-concealed smile played about her face as she put it at the top of the basket.

At four o'clock, we were at the landing. My new friend had been accustomed to a canoe from childhood; he came from a lake country. Miss Appleton at once put him at his ease by telling me that he and she were going to turn the tables on me, — that they were going to do the paddling, and treat the host as guest. As she knew the stream and he did not, she took the after paddling seat. I sat between them on the bottom of the canoe, with my hat lying by my side. The conversation was spasmodic, touching upon canoeing, the stream, the trees, the shadows. The full length of a canoe is not the best distance for continued conversation.

Young Cobb was a good paddler, and he knew it. He knew, too, that Ruth saw it. This source of satisfaction told upon him. His timidity wore off under it. His wit was not slow; and, encouraged by our occasional remarks or questions, his words came easily.

We had been paddling about half an hour, when Ruth declared that she was thirsty.

"Mr. Cobb," she said, "won't you open the basket there in the bow, and take out the flask that lies on the top and bring it down to me?"

He found it without difficulty, and stepped down toward me, with his paddle in one hand. I moved to let him by. The canoe gave a little lurch.

"Be careful, Mr. Robertson," she exclaimed, laughing, "or you'll have us upset. There, don't bother to come away by, but let me reach the flask over Mr. Robertson's head."

She reached forward to take it, throwing a shawl playfully around my shoulders as she did so. I wondered a little at it. She still held her paddle, and he held his. Neither alone could pull the drinking-cup from the bottom of the flask except after laying down the paddle.

"Hold on to the top, and I will pull the cup from the bottom," she said to him.

It stuck. They pulled hard, and then I felt something give way. On the moment the canoe gave a deep lurch to one side, and water came pouring into my eyes and mouth.

"We 're over!" I cried.

A rippling laugh came from over my head. I shook the water out of my eyes, and found myself sitting as before in the bottom of the canoe. Ruth and Cobb were shaking with laughter. The flask had broken in two directly above me.

The shawl had kept my clothes dry, but my face and hair were dripping. When I saw the broken flask, and realized what a spectacle I must present, I could not help laughing heartily at myself. Cobb joined more freely when he saw how I took it. From that moment we were all on the best of terms. A little wholesome laughter will break even the biggest barrier.

When we reached the place which we had chosen for luncheon, Cobb fell back into his old reserve. For a few moments I could not explain the change. I soon discovered, however, that he did not know just what to do with himself. It was contrary to his sense of propriety to lie back lazily while Miss Appleton spread the lunch. He was nervous to be doing something as his share of the work, and yet he dared not offer his clumsy fingers to help about the basket. While I was wondering what to do to put him at his ease, Ruth looked up at him.

"Oh, Mr. Cobb, have you a knife?"

"Yes. Would you like it?"

"I am going to ask you to do a very difficult piece of work. I did n't bring any knives or forks. We must have at least one of each, and you will have to whittle them for us. We can eat from our fingers; but I want a knife and fork for handling butter, sardines, and the like. Do you suppose you can make them?"

She was looking straight into his eyes, and smiling. I wondered whether a man could n't do anything under the sun if that girl looked at him so and asked him.

I knew now why she had left out the knives and forks.

"How wonderfully thoughtful you are!" I exclaimed, when he had gone to find the proper sticks for whittling.

"How sillily so! I want to say to myself. I did one frightfully silly thing to-day. Do you remember my asking you whether you objected to being a martyr for his sake? Well, like a silly child, I planned that ducking for you, — though not just in that way. I remembered that a good laugh is the best way to do away with stiffness. So I took a broken flask purposely, hoping to have some little fun out of it. I had to make you the victim, for I feared that he would think it unmannerly to laugh if I were the victim; but it turned out ever so much better than I expected. Yet I feel that it was very childish to make it deliberately at all."

"I don't see it so. It had just the effect you wanted."

"Yes; but it seems like deceiving him."

"No; for the actual happening — at any rate, my thinking that we had tipped over — was unpremeditated. It certainly was very funny. It goes to prove what I just said, — that you are wonderfully thoughtful."

Her only answer was a smile and a playful "Pooh!"

I suppose all New England country boys are experts with the jack-knife, or aspire to be. Whittling is almost the national perennial amusement. Cobb was no exception. Before the coffee was ready, he laid before Miss Appleton a slender, straight-bladed, flexible knife and two strong, three-pronged forks.

"How beautiful! Where did you learn to make such beauties?"

"I learned to make knives and forks on the Madawanipee River; I can't remember the time when I could n't whittle."

"I thought that you had but recently come to Madawanipee."

"That is true. I never tried to make a knife or fork before."

"Oh, then you not only learned the process, but discovered it as well."

Our luncheon was very simple, but it was eminently fitting, — a compliment merited by few luncheons put up by picnicking women. It was not composed one half of cake, one quarter of mashed pie, and the remainder of thick sandwiches which could not be bitten through. Everything was recognizable at first sight. The salad — I won't risk my literary reputation by trying to describe it — knew its place ; it had n't gone visiting among the wafers, pickles, and sugar.   The cake was not thirst-inspiring, and there was no needless loaf to carry back.

Miss Appleton sat on a little knoll, with her back against a tree.   Cobb sat upon a stone at her right hand; and I rested upon one elbow on the grass at her feet, happy, and caring only that they would not remind me that I was not young like them.

"How long have you been here?" Miss Appleton asked, turning to Cobb.

"About three months."

"Do you like the town?"

"Yes; it's very pretty. I am getting along pretty well here; and yet I ought to say, if I'm going to be frank, that I don't like it."

"How strange! It's pretty, and you are prosperous, and yet you don't like it."   She looked up into his face as if he were about to tell some very interesting story.

"I seem to be out of my element here," he said.   "I seem to live in an atmosphere that does n't agree with me. I 'm irritable, sour, what I believe you call cynical, all the time. I was never so at home."

124

"Tell me about your home, won't you? I love all New England towns."

"It is n't much of a town, — nothing but a hamlet; two stores, a blacksmith-shop, a saw-mill, a tavern, a church, and a dozen houses are all."

"That's all the more interesting. I think I can see the place now. On summer noons, not a sound is heard except the clatter of dishes when you pass a house, or the munching of a horse which crops the grass at the side of the road. It is quiet like that all day, is n't it, except for the occasional rattle of the big chain that draws logs up into the mill, or the occasional soothing buzz of a saw, or the ring of the blacksmith's anvil?"

"Yes; it is quiet always. Now and then a farmer's wagon rattles down the hill, or a mowing-machine clatters along the road; but most of the time it is perfectly still."

"Yes; as you spoke I could hear the creak of the whiffle-tree on the farmer's wagon and the click, click, click of the mowing-machine. Does the mill run by water?"

"Yes."

"And does the brook that feeds it flow through the hamlet, with a well-worn bridge over it?"

"Yes." He smiled at her guesses.

"I think I can see the village now. One can lie on the grass under the trees beside the road by the bank of the stream day after day, and watch the colors come and go, and hear and see the birds, and watch the grazing cattle, and see the people drive lazily by, and never hear a harsh sound, nor see a hideous thing, nor feel an ignoble impulse, nor know of vice or pain or struggle."

She had been speaking quietly and slowly, with her eyes fixed on the canoe. It lay half-hidden behind the bushes. For my mood there was a poem in its beautiful lines and in its graceful poise upon the water. He looked only at her. His face brightened as her imagination took her farther and farther into his old home.

"But tell me about the people," Ruth continued.

"There is nothing to tell. They are very

plain people, dressed in coarse, ill-fitting clothes; but they are honest." He spoke with something of pride; but as he went on his face darkened, and his tone became bitter. "They are awkward, bungling in everything they do. They never have any pleasure, as pleasure goes here. I suppose they cheat themselves into thinking they are happy, — in their ignorance; and I suppose they are no better than they ought to be, nor as good as they look."

He was not looking at her now; but she had watched him from the moment his tone changed.

"Do you know, I like to think of the people in these towns as well as to think of the towns themselves. They have such glorious freedom. A woman is in the middle of her washing, with her sleeves rolled above the elbows. If she wants to speak to a neighbor, out she goes. No dressing, — not even the sleeves turned down, — no windows and doors to lock, but just 'up and away.' In such places, people live their own lives in their own way. Little or nothing is done or left undone for fear of what 'people will say; ' and everybody helps everybody else. Is n't it so?"

"Yes, it must be admitted that's a thing people are generous of; they are generous of trouble, though far from it with respect to money."

" Tell me about the young women, or girls. There must be some about my age."

" Yes, there are two in the village; one is the school-teacher, and the other is the doctor's daughter. Well, the school-teacher is tall and dark, with black hair and small hands and—"

Miss Appleton interrupted him with a laugh.

" Would it make any difference if she were light and short, with red hair and small hands?"

I expected to see him close his shell again; but he seemed to enjoy her raillery.

" Why, no, I suppose not. But I thought you wanted to hear about her."

" So I do; but the length and breadth and color of her are not she. I would rather know what she reads and what she dreams and what she does with her time. But never mind. You are not much interested in the school-teachei yourself. Tell me about the doctor's daughter.

You may tell me about *her* height and hair and hands if you like."

"It does n't make much difference. She's tall, but light, and her hands and feet are not so small as the school-teacher's." He smiled, as if to describe her in such a way were superfluous. "I don't know what she thinks about; I could never altogether make out. Many days she takes a book out to the river in the morning, and does n't come back till night; but when she comes back, her eyes are very bright, and her face is very peaceful, — or if not altogether peaceful, her mouth is very firm, though it is never hard. And then other days she goes over to old Aunt Hannah's, as everybody calls her, and stays there all day, talking and reading out loud. Sometimes, when some of the people who live alone are sick, she goes with her father, and stays to nurse them. And then when there is n't any minister in town, she runs the Sunday-school."

"Tell me more about her." She looked into his face in a way that said even more than her words.

129

"There is n't much more to tell. She is a sort of ubiquitous spiritual force in the community. She always carries sunshine with her, and I was going to say" — he smiled at the mixed metaphor — "a sunshine that leaves a good taste in the mouth. As you said a few moments ago of the village itself, one knows nothing of vice or pain or struggle when she 's about."

"I am inclined to get angry at people who speak, or even think, slightingly of country life. So many of the noblest, kindest, purest lives are lived in our New England country villages, in what seems outwardly like emptiness! I should like to know this friend of yours."

"She did one very funny thing just before I came away. She had done something — I don't know what — that she blamed herself for. She said it was giving in to a temptation that made her hate herself. There was a little party that evening, and people came from all the country round. For us it was a great affair, though it would seem awfully small in Madawanipee. She cared very much about it, and had been looking forward to it for days ; but to punish herself, — or discipline herself, she called it, — she went home when the evening was only half over, and she was enjoying herself most. I told her it was silly ; but she said she was going to exercise her will-power in some wholesome discipline."

"I believe in that girl," Ruth said. "It may have been a silly thing to do, but it showed a spirit I like."

There was no mistaking Cobb's gratification. His face did not darken again ; not even embarrassment came into it again. There was an energy in it that I had not seen before since he first came to Madawanipee. He was himself again, — and it was almost a beautiful self.

IX.

IN quiet Madawanipee the function of a church is hardly less social than religious. On Sunday mornings everybody sees everybody else, if not at church, at least on the way.

The first Sunday in June was the most beautiful of the spring. There had been a slight rain during the night, but a breeze which had sprung up about daybreak had cleared the sky. The new-blown leaves were quivering in the ecstasy of life. The air was crisp, but not penetrating; every breath seemed to give new firmness and new energy to every part of body and soul. It was hard to pass within the church walls to dimness and heaviness of atmosphere and dignified confinement.

As the moment for beginning the service approached, I began to fear that Ruth was not coming; but soon I saw her face in the doorway. She brought the morning with her into the church. It was easy to wonder whether she had not even been the maker of the morning. Its calm energy but tender blitheness had their counterparts in her eyes, her cheeks, and her step. The church was no longer dim, nor its atmosphere heavy.

In response to the prayer before the sermon, a short aria was given. It seemed to be a very song of Nature. It began with the first breath of morning air, as one would sing on waking; then came the growing exhilaration, the eagerness of conscious vigor rising into higher and higher regions of activity; it closed with a mounting strain of aspiration. The music was new to me. I had heard nothing new so good for a long time.

At the close of the sermon, the preacher prayed that God would teach us about ourselves, and help us to hold to every fragment of truth and love and purity in our hearts. I watched Ruth's face, and saw that she joined the prayer with passionate earnestness. God had never seemed so great before. Even this girl, most true, most kind, most pure, was asking God to make her truer, kinder, purer; and she knew that he would do it. I cried out, almost aloud, unconsciously, "How great, O God, thou art!"

At the close of the service, I busied myself with my gloves in the hope that my delay would put me in Ruth's way. Before I reached the door, Cobb met me.

"Mr. Robertson," he said, "I can't thank you enough for yesterday. I feel like a new man to-day. Last evening I went out on the street, and everything looked different. Instead of wondering whether every man I saw was a rake and every woman a plaything, voluntary or involuntary, I found myself seeing the good things in their faces. If I saw a bundle in a man's hand, it seemed as if it must be a present for his child or wife or somebody, and not something that he wanted to hide. The letters which the girls were taking from the post-office were innocent schoolmate effusions, not secret flirtations by mail. I was almost optimistic; but I can afford to be so for awhile after so many weeks of cynicism. You and Miss Appleton set me free.   Best of all, what Miss Appleton said about the doctor's daughter put the solid ground under my feet.   When my morbid state had taken away my faith in my sister, life was pretty hard living."

Before we overtook Ruth, one of Cobb's employers came up and carried him off for dinner.   When I met her, she was unengaged.   I walked home with her.

To me the day had been wondrously beautiful, — the sunlight, the crisp air, the waving leaves, the song, the sermon, the prayer; and now, for a time at least, Ruth was mine.   It was one of the rich charms of the girl that her thoughts and sympathies were never alien to her companion.   I found her enthusiastic over the day and the service, except the music, which she did not appear to appreciate.

"Do you know who wrote it?" I asked.

"I believe it was an Agnes Wentworth."

The name staggered me.

"Have you ever heard it before?"

"Yes; they sang it often at the church I used to attend in Vermont."

"But tell me about the writer, if you can. Who is she?"

"She is a young woman who was educated in the public schools there."

"Do you mean that she is a young woman now?" I asked eagerly.

A half-smile played about her mouth.

"Yes," she answered; "she is a young woman now."

Her answer would have satisfied much of my curiosity, if her manner had not betrayed that the story was not half told.

"Do you know her?" I asked.

"Yes, pretty well," she answered with a smile.

"I really think the song was very beautiful, and I want to hear about the writer. Won't you tell me about her? Judging from your face, I am inclined to think that there is some mystery. Years ago, I knew a young woman of that name; and I am naturally interested to hear of this other one."

"There isn't much to tell. I wrote the song, and I signed it by my two middle names.

136

My mother liked the name Ruth, and my father wanted me to keep my mother's full name; so I was named Ruth Agnes Wentworth."

"Agnes Wentworth! Where did your mother live?" I asked almost breathlessly.

"Highbank, Vermont."

We were crossing a bridge over a brook which ran through the town. I stopped and leaned forward over the rail, looking into the water. I needed time to get my thoughts together. We had often stopped at the bridge before, and she thought nothing of my abruptness. She followed my example.

"You never mentioned Highbank before," I said.

"Haven't I? I have often spoken of the place, though perhaps not by name."

"Oh, I see. You always said 'in Vermont.' Do you know when your mother was born?"

"In eighteen thirty."

There was no further doubt. The morning's happiness was complete; 't was overflowing, so that I dared not look at her. On the night of the symphony concert, I had put down the dream that the new face was the old face come back to earth and to me ; yet it was true. The old face, the old voice, the old greatness of soul, had been repeated from the mother in the child to cheer my last years ; and the old love in my heart had gone forth to meet them.

Ruth seemed to respect my revery ; but at last she broke the silence : —

" You seem much interested in Highbank ; do you know the town ? "

" I lived there many years ; I went to school there."

" Did you know my mother ? "

" Yes. It seems incredible that you are her daughter. You are much like her, almost the image of her as she was forty years ago ; but I thought I knew all about her family. I did not know she had a daughter so much younger than herself; I thought your sister Kate your mother's youngest child."

" She was while she lived. I was born two years after Kate died."

" I was away from Highbank all those years; and though I knew when Kate died, I never heard of you." I did not tell her that for years I kept trace of all the happenings in her mother's life ; and then, finding that my heart, instead of healing, only grew sorer, I heard only such news as chanced to come to me. " Have you any relatives in Highbank now ? "

" Mrs. Arthur Thomas is my mother's youngest sister. Do you know her ? "

" Yes. I never knew that she was a Miss Wentworth. By the way, were you staying with her nine years ago this winter ? "

" Yes."

" Then you are the Ruth who gave the little shivering negro boy a sled-ride, and lent him a muff. Do you remember it ? "

" I remember it chiefly because a gentleman came to the house that evening to see Uncle Arthur, and spoke kindly about it. Are you the gentleman ? "

" Yes. Do you know that though you have been here but six months or so, I owe to you much of the pleasure that I have had in Mada-wanipee during the seven or eight years that I have been here ? "

"How can that be?"

"When I saw you at Highbank, I discovered how interesting some children can be. I wondered afterward whether others would not be interesting if I could only get to know them. I immediately set to work to find out. I picked up acquaintance with a good many children here, and have found in their freshness and heartiness both moral and intellectual help."

As I spoke, I wondered whether every beautiful thing in my life had not come through either Agnes or Ruth. I fell into revery, — such revery as one falls into during perfect happiness and in perfect companionship. For several moments neither of us spoke.

"I am going to Highbank this week," she said meditatively. "I doubt whether I come back here at all. Mr. Loring is coming Tuesday, and Mrs. Loring does not need my company any longer."

I did not realize just what she had said. I only knew that now, just as she was more to me than ever before, more than I had dreamed that she could ever be, she told me that she was to drop out of my life.

Quick as the impulse, I cried out.

"Oh, my Ruth, I can't let you go now!"

She turned suddenly to look at me. I had never seen her much moved before. Her face had lost its light; for once I saw it without sympathy. She looked at me without seeming to see me. She looked dazed, as if she had just seen some awful thing, and was trying to grasp the idea of it. In a moment or two her face cleared; the light of sympathy came back. Without speaking, she looked at me kindly, wonderingly, almost pityingly.

"Pardon me," I pleaded; "I spoke on impulse. You cannot know how much of new life you have brought me, how much of new faith, of new aspiration; for even an old man may have his aspirations. To all that you had done for me you just added the vivid memory, I may almost say the representation, of what is dearest to me in Highbank, — young manhood and womanhood there; and it was you who opened my eyes to know fondness for children, — perhaps the greatest pleasure of my last eight years. Now you tell me that you are about to go away; so I cried out impulsively that I could not let you.   Forgive me!"

Her face brightened.   Doubtless her thought was different from mine, but I could not feel despondent when I saw brightness in her face. I was almost willing to trust my moods to her. I felt that if I had reason to be despondent her keen sympathy would know it.   Even before she spoke, I knew that there must be hope for me.

"But you go to Highbank sometimes; and there you see all the old scenes, and won't need me to represent them.   And, besides, you will come to see me at my uncle's; and perhaps we can take some walks or rides as we have done here, and you can show me your favorite bits of Nature.   You will tell me about my mother as a girl, too, so far as you knew anything about her."

X.

ON the afternoon before Ruth's departure from Madawanipee, I called upon her. Though we had been together so much, or perhaps because we had been together so much, I had never called upon her before. I smiled at the thought of an old man like myself making a formal call upon a young girl. I had never been much given to calling; and as the years went on, I became more and more averse to it. The sensation was almost new. As I left home, I thought of my first call as a young man in Highbank. I smiled at my youthful terror lest my long legs, my hat, my gloves, and my arms should not distribute themselves in due form about my corner of the room. It had seemed so presumptuous to take off my overcoat, as if I were an expected guest, that in spite of warnings from all the authorities I respected, I had worn it into the parlor. Somehow we never do a thing easily until we have done it often, or unless we have seen so much of the world that the mere doing of new things has become an old story. To my bashfulness, everything new was awful to contemplate just because it was new.

As I approached Mrs. Loring's house, I felt much as if I were going to my own funeral. Certainly a part of me was to be buried; and there was to be nothing picturesque in it, as there had been in the funeral of myself which I had once dreamed about. Yet even this ceremony had one bright feature, — I was expected. When the bell rang at sharp three o'clock, Ruth would know that it was I. For the day, at least, I was to hold a place in her thoughts strictly my own. I felt a bit of pride that I was a person of so much importance that the much-sought Miss Appleton wished me to come to her by appointment. Even sorrow, unless it has become almost despair, cannot bury our vanity.

At my entrance, she laid down a notebook, which apparently she had been studying.

"It was very good of you to come," she said.

"I try always to be good to myself," I answered.

"And to other people?"

"Some other people."

"I hope you number me among them. If you do, I shall ask lots of things of you. Do you want my parting instructions?"

"Surely. It is very good of you to leave even so much of yourself behind."

"But they are not myself, you know; they have chiefly to do with other people."

"I can hardly fancy your giving instructions which are not parts of yourself. You put yourself into all you do; so I shall find you in whatever you are so good as to leave for me to do."

"I'm not going to leave you much; but you have kindly helped me in so many things which I have tried to do that I have taken it for granted that you will keep up your part of them after my part stops."

This little speech was the pleasantest thing that I had ever heard her say, and I cannot help putting it down in black and white to stand to my credit after I am gone. I had not only helped her, as it was my one eager joy to do, but I had done my part so well that she did not know that it was chiefly for her sake that I did it.

" I believe Frank Murphy at the jail," she continued, " is in a fair way to become a man at last, after all these years of mere animal life; and his friend who spoke to you the day you went with me seems to have a good deal of purpose, and of grit, as well. Won't you go to see them, to keep up their courage, sometimes?"

" Most gladly; but will they see me, and keep up my courage?"

" What do you mean?"

" Won't they be so lonesome at losing you that they will only despise a man like me for a friend?"

" Of course not. What they want is sympathy, — not pity or patronage, but a sense that somebody wants them to succeed in getting upon a new plane, believes that they will succeed, and will give them a hand of friendship and encouragement now and then. You can do that."

" I can do all you say, but I can't make them feel that I do it. I can't make them feel my sympathy as you do; and, besides, I fear that I have n't so much. You don't know the power you have for doing good in the world. You must not suspect that every one can do what you can. You can't realize that to the ordinary mortal you seem like a being from another world, —all sympathy, all kindness, all hopefulness, all purity, all graciousness. You can do more good by your mere temporary presence among people than I could do, even though I were a woman myself, in a score of visits. Pardon me for speaking so plainly, — I 'm a blunt old man, you know, — but I don't want you to let your power go unused through ignorance. You have infinitely more of all that makes noble womanhood an inspiration than any other woman I know. So don't expect too much from me, in the way of accomplishment, at least; you can't expect too much in the way of endeavor, for I 'll try anything you ask."

"Now you make me feel uncomfortable," she said, with a puzzling smile. "I feel that I have either been deceiving you on the one hand, or if not, that I have been a ' wicked and slothful servant.' But never mind; I'm going to leave another bit of work for you, if you'll take it."

"Certainly I shall. But again I must warn you not to expect too much; for I still insist that you have a power that few in the world can have to help people. Neither, I think, have you neglected your opportunities. If you should do nothing for your own development by such a broad life as you are leading, you would soon lose that power. The first requisite for such power is a broad field of personal interests. So please don't think I was asking you to lose yourself in work for others; I only wanted to remind you that because of your own self-care you have so much more power to care for others."

"It's very kind of you to encourage me so; but in spite of what you say I shall expect more from you than I have myself accomplished. The second case is a telegraph messenger boy, Johnny Hardy. He has the making of a strong man in him. I have been helping him to pick up something of an education during his spare time.

Will you help him in the same way after I have gone?"

"He won't want me. He will think it a bore to come to see me and seek for help. He will think me an old fogy; and after two or three trials he will stop coming. But I can tell you whom he will like as a guide; that's my nephew, Harry Templeman. He has taken a good deal of interest in Johnny already, especially of late; and Johnny likes him. Let me send him around to see you this evening, so that you can instruct him in his duties. He will be overjoyed to take, in any fashion, your place."

"I fear he would spoil Johnny. I don't mean do him harm; but I fear that he would not keep him up to the mark. Johnny has told me something of their sudden friendship, — if I may call so unequal a thing a friendship; and, if I may speak so freely of your nephew, I begin to suspect the genuineness of it all. Your nephew is n't conscious of the reasons for his sudden interest in Johnny; and I fear that he will discover them by and by, and will then regret the bargain he makes with me. So I should prefer that you would take my place."

"But, pray, how do you know so much about my nephew's motives, — more than he does?"

"Women often see things that men do not see. Men must reason a thing out, and so must have well-verified premises and other equipments of logic. Women just *see*. To be sure, many, perhaps most of them, often see what is n't there to be seen, just as most men often reason wrongly; but many of them see truly."

"I should like to know this mystery of Harry's attitude toward Johnny."

"But I 'm not likely to tell you," she laughed. "He may tell you himself, when he discovers it."

"Then I must help him discover it."

"Oh, no; that would never do. You would surely betray how your curiosity was excited; and that would involve me. Imagine the position you would put me in by letting him know that I thought I understood him better than he understands himself! So you will please say

150

nothing about it to him, and take Johnny under your own supervision. He has no relatives here, and needs supervision."

She was sitting in a large easy-chair, leaning well back, with her feet half stretched out before her. Her cheek rested against the back of her chair, as her deep blue eyes looked at me. She was clothed — but I never can describe a woman's dress. Yet one thing always impressed me : other women looked as if they had clothes made, and then somehow got inside of them ; her clothes seemed so distinctly to belong to her that one could not think of them as existing by themselves. With her a change of gown was like a change of expression, or of color, or of mood. Clothing seemed never to add or take away or alter her. In all garbs she was just herself.

Her arm, with its long firm hand, lay stretched out on the table at her side. Her fingers were toying with a new book on Plato. She seemed to me an embodiment in repose of all that was beautiful in life. There was about her a sense of power that prepared one for any accomplishment when activity began again.

Before her, in the corner of the room, stood a piano, covered with music, — Wagner, Chopin, Beethoven, Haydn, - Bach. Photographs of a few of the world's masterpieces of painting were upon the walls, and half-a-dozen casts stood about the room.

The world's treasures of highest thought, in all lines of manifestation, were open to her, and she knew how to use them. Had she chosen, her beauty, shining out of her heart into her face, could command admirers anywhere. Yet she was unconscious of everything but the little ragamuffin in the street, Johnny Hardy, telegraph messenger No. 3.

She left me for a moment to get a few memoranda connected with the work which she was to leave to me. While she was gone, the little girl who had flirted with me in church, and had asked in the garden for the "birdie song," strayed into the room. When she saw me, she started to withdraw; but I coaxed her back. She seemed half to remember me. She had a pencil and paper in one hand and a sketch-book in the other.

" Do you draw pictures ? " I asked.

" Yeth 'm ; Wuth ith learnin' me."

" Do you draw pictures in the big book ? "

" No 'm. Wuth dwaws in it, an' 'en I twy to dwaw the thame fing on a paper."

" Won't you let me see what you 've done ? "

She approached timidly at first, but courage soon came.

" I did it all mythelf, an' Wuth did n't do none."

She showed me a picture of a very rickety table. Perhaps with the aid of a little stiffening it would make a capital clothes-horse.

" Here ith what Wuth did," she explained, handing me the sketch-book.

" Oh, I 'll let you thee a funny picture that Wuth made the other day about thpillin' thum water."

She turned the pages clumsily, and finally showed me myself drenched with water, while Ruth and my friend Cobb were holding their sides with laughter. The likenesses were excellent. But I was more interested in the sketch on the opposite page. It pictured me of gigantic

153

stature, with a group of thin-faced, flat-chested, slim-limbed dwarfs looking up at me. My picture was drawn in ink; but the others were done in pencil, as if by after-thought.

The child saw what I was looking at.

"The big man ith a good man; an' the other men want to be good like him tho they can be big like him."

"How do you know that?" I asked.

"Becauth Wuth tol' me the little men wanted to be big like the big man, but could n't unleth they did like he did. Wuth dwew the little men one day jus' for me."

"You 'll be a big man some day, won't you?"

"No 'm," she answered eagerly, and with snapping eyes; "I 'm goin' to be a big woman."

"Is that better than being a big man?"

"Courth! It ith better than anyfing elth in the world; Wuth tol' me tho."

Though Ruth came in while I was looking at the sketch-book, she made no comment; but the sketch and all it meant to me remained fresh in memory. A man does n't forget that sort of tribute, off-hand though it be.

154

Before I went, I chanced to comment upon the volume of Plato with which she was toying, and our conversation turned to her reading of philosophy. I had never suspected the variety of her interests.

"Do you care much for philosophy?" I asked.

" Yes, I try to read more or less in it; but the field is so enormous, and one's time is so limited!"

" I did n't suppose women cared much for that sort of thing. Woman's field is intuition, not logic."

" You talk as if they were incompatible," she answered, with an amused smile.

" They seldom or never go together."

"What heresy you talk! They 're like man and wife."

" Yes; he 's the logic, and she 's the intuition."

"Oh, no! I shall have to change my figure. They 're like mountain-trail and carriage-road; the trail is shorter and more interesting, but the carriage-road is more dignified, — and safer."

"I suppose in your philosophy you always take the short cut."

"Yes; but I generally go back and make the trip over again by the road. I like to see how stupid and slow and dull you men can be. I could cut straighter roads myself sometimes, and perfectly safe ones, too."

"I suppose I shall have to believe you. I have seen evidence enough of it myself; but you are the first woman I ever knew, I think," — I had to add "I think," for I could not grant her unqualified superiority to Agnes even in this, — "who added to a wonderful intuition a head for logic.

"To-day is a proper time for philosophy," I continued, as I rose to go, "for I am sadly in need of it. What word has your philosophy for one who is fated to be wofully lonesome, as I shall be after you have gone?"

"I am afraid," she answered, smiling sympathetically, "that it can only say that you should n't bind your hopes to earthly things."

"That's the logical part of your philosophy. What does intuition say?"

"It says that if you are lonesome here, you ought to go back to your old home, among old friends, in Highbank."

"And young friends?"

"I was n't thinking about them, — very much," she added conscientiously.

"I was. I suspect that if I return there, it will be because they, and not the old friends, draw me."

She held out her hand. As I held it, and looked into her eyes, I forgot that I was supposed to go. I was recalled to myself by feeling her fingers slipping from my grasp.

I wonder how, when I reached the sidewalk, I knew which way to turn.

XI.

I HAD chosen the afternoon for my farewell with Ruth, because she was going to a musicale in the evening, and I could not be satisfied with the few moments of time and the few words of commonplace parting which we could have in crowded rooms.

As the evening wore on, however, I was unbearably restless. It was possible that I might never see her again; but I might see her once more now if I would, for I had an invitation to the musicale. I knew, however, that there would be no comfort in such a meeting.

About nine o'clock, I closed my book and went out for a short walk. Half-unconsciously, like a business man who finds himself on a holiday wandering toward his office, I turned my steps toward the house of Mrs. Pembroke, the giver of the musicale. When I reached there, I told myself that, since I had been invited, I had the privilege of taking all I could get of the entertainment; but I would not go in. I compromised by walking about the house several times. The windows were open, and the curtains were up. For a solace to my conscience, as it were, I fingered my invitation-card. As I passed down a narrow street by the side, I caught a glimpse through the window of Ruth. She was standing, talking with a younger, shorter girl. Her hair was arranged — no; there was no arrangement about it; it seemed to have grown so. It parted loosely, falling naturally at either side of the brow, — a natural crown, more glorious than any that goldsmith ever made. Her gown was of dark, soft silk, with a tiny golden figure. It was trimmed with ribbon of a golden yellow. Strange though it may seem, that vision of radiance reconciled me for all time to hideous gowns. If it were a part of the code of dress that none but radiantly beautiful women should wear bright, dazzling gowns, not even they would wear them. No woman would dare to challenge criticism by declaring by her dress that she thought herself beautiful. So, as I looked at Ruth, I praised the women who have no sense of the fitness of things. I can even look with complaisance at a gown which makes a plain woman hideous; I realize that it contributes its mite to Ruth's privilege of giving our eyes a feast.

The girl who was talking to her seemed unconscious that there was anything in the world but they two, for Ruth's whole self appeared intent upon the other's words. In her clear, kindly eye, strong, tender mouth, and ready smile, one seemed to see an infinite force, eager in sympathy. The face of the other girl, as Ruth looked down into it, was transfigured. I needed no better proof that her power was not a figment of my imagination; others felt it as well as I.

While I was watching, opposite the window, I heard steps approaching. I sauntered slowly on, taking a turn around the square.

When I reached the front of the house, Ruth was near a window on that side. She was talking to a young man of rather unsavory reputation. He was commonly called a handsome fellow, and was very popular, apparently, with the girls of the town. I had watched him often. I had seen him look hard into girls' faces with his insinuating smile, as much as to say, " You are bound to be interested in what I say, because it is I who say it." I had seen him look hard, almost fiercely, into the faces of other girls, as if to try their wills against his, — as if to dare them to refuse to grant him a favor. There was nothing of either sort in his face now. He seemed to know that he was with a girl who was to be neither flattered nor frightened; yet her manner was as I had always seen it, — gracious, sympathetic, cordial. He seemed to feel that her sympathy was with his better self, and that with his common self she had nothing to do, — refused to have anything to do. I had never seen his face so manly before. Her mere presence was enough to bring to the surface the best in him.

Mrs. Pembroke had been kind-hearted toward her children, and had allowed the older ones to stay up for the evening. They passed through the room, and Ruth called them to her. Her companion soon went off, and they arranged themselves for a story. The youngest, a boy, sat on her lap, with his light hair resting on her shoulder; his frank, eager eyes were upturned to hers. The younger girl, dark-haired, with rich, rounded features, stood on a footstool at her side. The older girl, with flaxen hair, clear-cut, almost thin features, sat on a footstool at her knee, and with elbows resting in Ruth's lap looked up into her face. The group served well to show Ruth's beauty. The characteristics of the three childish faces were combined in her own, — the frankness and eagerness of the boy, the richness of abounding health and spirits of the younger girl, the intellectual acuteness and spirituality of the older. Her face had in it a wonderful comprehensiveness, a something which I have tried in vain to name, —a something indicative of a peculiar largeness of nature.

It is not strange that as I watched her, realizing always that in a few hours she would be gone, perhaps gone out of my life forever, I felt that everything left behind was small and mean.

I dreaded the days when every street-corner, every road, every turn of the stream, would speak eloquently of her, and no one would be left behind to inspire new hopes and new endeavors.

A few drops of rain brushed my cheek. I hailed them eagerly. It had been clear early in the evening, and I knew that few of Mrs. Pembroke's guests would be prepared for rain. I hurried home, and returned ready for service. But the weather was fitful; and when Ruth came out, with Harry at her side, it was not raining. Since they were unprotected, I followed near enough to reach them if the shower should return, but beyond the sound of their voices. At Mrs. Loring's door, Harry left her; but before he had regained the street, I heard her call him back.

I plodded home alone in the dark and the wet.

XII

EARLY in the summer I betook myself to Highbank. I had often to confess to myself that the new interest which had come into my life was not easily to be disposed of. After a score or more of years in which the society of none had been indispensable to my happiness,—ay, even important,—I now found myself dependent upon this young girl. At first I blamed myself for this dependence. I told myself that I would conquer it. It seemed so weak and undignified to wander about the country after her! As a matter of moral discipline, I could not afford to yield to the craving. I soon gave up that high ground; I was too old to need training. If one must deny oneself even into old age, when is to come unfettered enjoyment? The rest of my life would be too short to require severe discipline; so I yielded.

When the train drew into Highbank, about

nine o'clock in the evening, a heavy mist, half rain, half fog, enveloped the town. Every distant object was magnified. The men and women wandering about the platform were Titanic in size. Faces were indistinct; it was such a night that in war men might take friend for foe, or foe for friend.

While I stood on the platform trying to decide where to take up my quarters, I heard the down train whistling around the curve just above the station. As I turned to watch the headlight stream through the fog, I caught sight of a figure which reminded me of Ruth. The back was toward me; but as I drew nearer, I thought I recognized Ruth's mackintosh and the hat which was her favorite on stormy days. Just as the engine of the train reached the end of the platform, she slipped. She tried to recover herself, but apparently caught her foot in her gown, and fell over upon the track. As she fell, her face turned toward me, and I thought I saw Ruth's eyes looking in horror at the approaching light.

I fear that I am not very brave nor very

quick. I am too likely to take it for granted that people who get into difficulties will get out alone much better than if confused by the proffer of aid. Yet when I saw Ruth fall, I had no such prudential thoughts. It seemed as if it was I who was in danger, and as if I alone could ward it off.

I dropped my luggage, and sprang for the track. There was no time to lift or even drag her. I could only half push, half roll her as she attempted to regain her feet. She had half risen; my thrust sent her prostrate upon the track beyond. I saw that she was safe.

The next that I knew I was here in the hospital. I opened my eyes as from a long but troubled sleep, and looked out upon the housetops. I saw the dear old steeple, into the belfry of which I used to climb when a boy, and I saw the clock-tower of the High School. Then, from the relative positions of those landmarks, I realized where I was. Soon came the dim remembrance of an on-rushing railroad train, of Ruth's danger, of my sudden spring, her second fall, a blow; and then all was a blank.

No one was in the room, and I could satisfy myself of my condition only by making a personal examination. I soon found that not all of my ribs were just as they should be, and one leg lay like a log. Suddenly I felt the shock all over again, and lost myself.

When I again awoke, the chair at my side was rocking gently, as if some one had but then left it, and a paper was lying on it. I picked up the paper, and read. Among the items was the following : —

"Last evening as the 8.45 northern train was drawing into the station, Miss Maggie Haggerty, a laundress who has been in the employ of James Upton, slipped upon a banana-peel, and fell upon the track. An elderly gentleman, apparently a stranger in town, ran to her assistance, and pushed her from the track, but could not make his own escape. He was struck by the pilot of the approaching train, and thrown several yards. He was taken to the Highbank hospital. Several of his ribs were broken, and it is feared that he is suffering from severe internal injuries. He was still unconscious at one o'clock this morning. Letters and papers found on his clothing make it clear that his name is Alfred Robertson, but his residence is unknown."

The paper bore date July 23. On a calendar which hung on the wall opposite, all the days of the month up to the twenty-sixth had been crossed with a lead pencil. I had apparently been unconscious nearly four days, for the sun was now low.

As soon as I had rested from the reading, I re-read the notice. Fortunate Maggie Haggerty! How little you know by how slight a thread your life hung! The dimming mist saved you. I fear, and it shames me to confess it, that, if I had not mistaken you for Ruth, my policy of non-interference would have prevailed. Your life would have paid.

XIII.

AS I have lain quietly here in the hospital, I have wondered that I ever called a hospital a place of horrors, or even a place of shadows, — a place to shrink from. As a boy, the mere approach to the building seemed to me an intense but tenderly given "Hush!" from some sad-eyed watcher. Pain and deformity and death lived here. My imagination felt the surgeon's knife, the cripple's want of power, the awfulness of the presence of death. In my childish thought, the activity of the body was the larger part of life. I felt that I could never be maimed, or even seriously ill; I should not be I, if my body had lost any of its powers. I had been told that to lose the power to think was to lose identity. It must be equally true that a boy who could not play ball and run and skate and jump could not be I. Uncanny indeed was the place where identity and even life might be lost.

One day I wondered how great were the ills that people bore here. I distrusted the strength of my imagination. I drew a pin from the corner of my waistcoat, and pressed it against my arm. I shut my teeth hard, and clenched my hand. I pressed the pin harder and harder, until an involuntary sigh escaped me, and then I threw it from me. The next moment I pitied myself for my weakness. Yet when I looked at my arm and saw the puncture tinged with blood, I dreaded to repeat the experiment. Did I fear the pain, or did I fear to maltreat and deface my own body? I never knew; for to me every scar and deformity, even the slightest, was uncanny. When I looked up at the hospital windows, my imagination had been strengthened. I knew that heroes lived there; and then a new wonder and a new terror seized me. I did not know how many people were within, but I knew that hundreds had been there. Were heroes so common? Oh, if not, if some who entered there were not heroes, how terrible a thing was life!

I wandered slowly away to the edge of the

hill, and looked far out over the valleys and the low-lying hills to the mountains. They had stood for centuries noble and untroubled. Should man, who was greater even than the mountains, live in fear of suffering? Then came the thought that drove away forever the shadows hovering over the building. The world was not full of heroes, nor yet was life a terrible thing; the suffering could make us heroes. The evil not only carried its own cure, but left a blessing behind. From that day, the hospital was a place where heroes were made; it was horrible only for those who proved to have nothing even of the making of heroes in them.

Now I am here. How changed my ideas of the place since I was a boy! When I go out, if I ever do, I shall be a cripple. I shall walk no more. Yet I smile when I think of the old fancy that to become a cripple is to lose identity. To be sure, there is much in the hospital methods that makes one wonder whether one is one's self; but it is rather amusing than otherwise. They have ticketed my bed with my name, address, ailment, treatment, and the like, as if I were already but a thing, unable to identify itself. George Talcott, an old school-mate whom I came to see here occasionally, used to say that he felt already labelled for the other world: he wondered only that his sins had not been enumerated on the tag for Saint Peter's benefit. As he had always lived in a family, he felt here the lack of personal interest to which he had been accustomed. He felt himself converted into a machine. Yet I find that I rather like this mechanical method: it seems to emphasize the comparative insignifi-cance of the physical body. One realizes, per-haps for the first time, how little one is depend-ent upon it.

I hear the roll of wheels on the way to the operating-room; I hear the clink of bottles, the hurrying of nurses, the anxious voices of in-quiring friends; I hear a nurse laughing and chatting in the hall; I hear the prattle of chil-dren's voices from another ward; I hear the tread of burdened steps from the ambulance to the outer door, and even as the stretcher passes my room I hear a doctor's laugh. What does it all mean ? Suffering is here, gayety is there ; but something greater than either is everywhere. Ask the man who has just been brought from the ambulance what is oftenest in his mind. It is not the pain which he has borne, nor that which he has yet to bear : it is the wife who is anxious for him, and the child who shudders at the thought of what has befallen him ; it is the loss of time and money which this accident entails, — time and money which should have gone to ease the wife's labors, to educate the child, to make home brighter. Ask the child whose laugh I heard why she laughed. It was not relief from pain, or the thought of escaping from a dreary hospital: it was the thought of home, of loving ones ; or it was the pleasant word of some passer-by, or a deed of some true-hearted child in story. Go the rounds, if you will; you will find life not much different here from what it is elsewhere. It is a little more intense, only, because the chances which befall the body here influence so powerfully human relationships. Our thoughts, our aims, our aspirations, our courage, our strength, our affections, — which are our real selves, — hospitals cannot mar; rather, hospitals help them.

I hope that I am not too optimistic. I hope that I have said not only what might be, but what is, true. Perhaps I am prejudiced; I have had so full a life, even in this confinement, that I suspect that others have fared in the same way. But why should I? Others have no Ruth!

One morning, a week after the accident, I was lying listlessly with my face toward the open door. A whispered consultation was holding just out of sight in the corridor.

"Then there is no immediate danger, and he can stand seeing people?"

"Yes. The danger that we fear may not manifest itself for a month yet."

In a moment Ruth entered my room.

"You are a naughty man," she exclaimed, with one of the smiles which I had been for weeks longing to see. "You said you would come to see me when you came to Highbank. You have been in town almost two weeks, and have n't been to see me yet. Are n't you ashamed of yourself? You see I won't let you free from your bargain, and so I have come to see you, instead."

She held my hand while she spoke.

"Yes; I am very much ashamed of myself, but I am not without my excuse. Do you remember once saying that you always had an uncomfortable sensation on looking at broken things, — shattered crockery, broken fences, tumbled-down houses, abandoned, broken-ribbed vessels? You could hardly expect an abandoned, broken-ribbed vessel like me to thrust himself in your sight. To be sure, I fear that I should not have gone to see you even if you had not told me about that old broken-ribbed vessel at Harpswell, but at least I have that excuse."

"No, I can't accept that as an excuse. I should n't have known that you were in such shape unless you had told me, — which you would n't have done, — and so I could not have been pained."

"No; but I must have limped from my injury. I might counterfeit any kind of limp, perhaps, well enough to deceive ordinary people, but you, with your woman's intuition, and in spite of an obvious *non-sequitur*, would at once know that I had a broken rib or two."

" What sublime confidence you have in your own theories about other people! Don't you want me to tell your fortune ? "

" I almost believe that you could. Do you remember your prediction about your little telegraph boy ? You saw a future in him, though no one else did, and it seems to be beginning, already."

" But I could n't tell a hero's fortune, — a real hero. And you know that is what every one calls you, now."

" Heaven forbid! If they only knew how cowardly I was ! "

"Ah, but you did it ! The bravest man may have most fear ; he is bravest because he faces not only danger, but fear beside."

" Unfortunately I did not face the fear. I was cowardly. Let's not talk about it. Only don't think me in any sense a hero. I was really basely cowardly."

" I can't let you talk so about yourself. It was a grand thing to do, to risk your life for some one you never saw before, — a girl that nobody knew."

She took my hand, thin and wrinkled with age and with sickness, and held it while she looked into my eyes and praised me. But for me there was only distress in the words, the caress, and the look ; and yet those were the first words of praise and that was the first caress I had ever had from a woman I loved.

" Oh, my child, how little you know of what was in my mind! I — thought — the — girl — was — you ! "

Once more the look of fright — seeming to ask " What have I done ? " — came into her face as on that Sunday afternoon in Madawanipee when I begged her not to go away. But now it was not a look of pity that followed it. There was quiet triumph in her face. Her heart could not fail to quicken when she knew that a man had risked his life for her, — and for her not simply as a woman, but because she was herself.

Yet, as always, she put aside all selfishness, and gave her thought to her companion. She turned from her own triumph to my distress.

"It was a heroic thing to risk your life for any one, friend or stranger. And you would have done it just the same if you had known that it was not I."

"No, my dear; I cannot flatter myself with any such thought. I believe that I should not; I am too cowardly. The fear of violence grows with the years of immunity from it. I despise myself as fully as if I had let the girl die, for I did not risk anything to save her. All the risk was taken for you. Nor was it brave to try to save you. I could not help it. Is it heroic to save one's head at the expense of one's arm? When I saw you fall, as I thought, I felt that it was I who fell, —that the train was about to crush out my life. Of course I tried to prevent that. So please don't talk of bravery or heroism any more. Let's forget it."

"I fear you're not likely to forget the accident soon. How long are they going to keep you in bed?"

"Nobody knows. At least, so they say. I may be out in a month; I may end my days here. But tell me how you happened to know about my being here?"

"The papers have been giving daily bulletins about you. It was not until yesterday, however, that I chanced to see your name. They wouldn't let me in here yesterday afternoon, because I came so late. So I had to wait till this morning. Tell me how you are this morning."

"I have grown rapidly better since I received my first morning caller. It cheers me up."

"I am glad if people come to see you. It tends to make life here much more endurable, I suppose. Do you have many callers?"

"I have had but one, so far."

"I hope that one comes often, then."

"I hope she will, for she does me a great deal of good."

She looked down at me with a questioning smile.

"Yes," I continued; "you are my first visitor. But I know that you have many demands on your time, and so I'm going to look upon this visit, and the next, if I get another, as especially great favors, to be grateful for always."

"Will you be grateful for more than one other visit?"

"Not only that, but the gratitude will grow as the square of the number of visits."

"I believe, then, that I never had so good an opportunity to win gratitude. I have half a mind to try to see how much I can win. How fast it would grow, — one, four, nine, sixteen, twenty-five, thirty-six, forty-nine, sixty-four! How jolly! Are you sure your gratitude will hold out?"

"Sure."

"I think I'd like to run up as far as sixty-four, any way, so I'll try it."

And she has, and a good deal farther. I am beginning to think that my gratitude is increasing as the cube of the number of visits. It seems to be approaching infinity very rapidly.

XIV.

I DID not depend on Ruth alone for youthful spirits. Soon after I came to Highbank, Harry followed me. I was not surprised when he appeared at the hospital.

"Well, my boy," I asked, "what are you doing in Highbank?"

"I'm doing several things. I'm looking after you, for one thing."

"Very kind; but you can't deceive me by such a statement as that. I know that you are a stickler for proper climaxes. You put the least important thing first. Go on with the list of purposes in Highbank."

"I am getting a change of air and scene, for another thing, — and that's anti-climax."

"To be sure. For that very reason I know that you mean more than you seem. What's the particular change of scene that you need?

181

Is it necessary that Miss Appleton's face shall be in your scenery?"

"I rather suspect that I am in need of that particular change of scene."

"If she is the object lacking in your scenes, you have come to the right place. She comes here to see me nearly every day. She will be here in about an hour."

"If I were only an egotistic fatalist," he laughed, "I should say that you had been subjected to this accident especially for my benefit, so that I should have plenty of chances to see her. Has she been good to you?"

"I wonder at your asking. To have her near, to hear her voice, to see her listening while one talks, to watch her smile, is enough to make one call her good to one. Though she does nothing, she is somehow an inspiration."

"Yes; that's why I'm here, — I need a little inspiration."

"Do you expect to get it?"

"I expect to get a certain kind of inspiration every time I look at her. It is worth while going a long way just to watch a beautiful woman.   Yet there is one kind of inspiration which I fear I won't get from her; yet I go on hoping."

"I supposed you found out long ago whether she would give it to you."

"No; but I mean to find out pretty quick."

"If you wait here long enough, you can find out to-day.   She will be here soon.   I think she would n't be afraid to tell you in my presence."

He looked up quickly.

"Do you mean that?" he asked.

"I mean that I think so.   She has given me no indication, one way or the other."

"I'm going to look her up to-day.   Where is she likely to be?"

"She'll be here in an hour; then you can meet her by accident."

"Thank you, no.   I would rather have her know that I met her by intention."

"Then go to Mr. Thomas's house."

He spent a little time before my mirror, and then went out.

The day was extremely hot. The wind had blown for nearly a week from the scorching plains of the interior. About three o'clock, almost without warning, a heavy gale reached the town, and brought with it torrents of rain. I gave up the expectation of seeing Ruth. I was glad that she was too sensible to venture out. Then I began to wonder whether it was not Harry, rather than the storm, who kept her away. I began to fear.

The wind and the rain were over by six o'clock. About seven, much to my surprise, Ruth appeared.

"I am glad that you did n't do anything so foolish as to venture out this afternoon," I said, by way of greeting.

"But I did; I was out in the storm an hour, and I came very near the hospital in the midst of it. I have a new patient."

"Who is it?"

"A girl whom I came across yesterday. She is very ill, and she has a young child to care for. I put her in charge of a dear old lady near here."

184

" Did you know her before ? "

" By name only.   She is the granddaughter of an old friend of my father.   She is an outcast.   The man she loved deserted her six months ago.   She was never married."

" How did you happen across her ? "

" It 's a story that I am ashamed of.   She came to me last evening, and told me who she was and what her life had been.   She expected me to help her find some work and put her on her feet again.   She said she did n't care so much for herself, but the thought of her child drove her to appeal even to a stranger like me.   The notion of helping such a girl to her feet rather took my breath away.   I knew that all my friends would shun her, and would be inclined to shun me too if I had anything to do with her.   I tried to cheer her, but could n't bring myself to make any personal sacrifice for her.   I knew of an institution, or ' home,' for such as she, and gave her money to get there. I compromised with my conscience by taking her to the railroad station in our own carriage. I did n't feel called upon to do anything further.

Oh, it was outrageous! I treated her like another sort of being."

She paused. Her brow clouded. I had never seen contempt on her face before.

I knew, nevertheless, that I had heard only a part of the story. I had come to have absolute confidence in her. Probably to others my faith would have seemed extravagant; but I might almost say that it was the growth of forty years. It was so great that I suspect that I should have trusted her even though I had seen her doing something contrary to every letter of the moral law. Her intuition was so nearly unerring, her love of all that is best was so strong, that she seemed superior to those laws and restraints that we weaker mortals need, — like fences to keep us out of our neighbors' fields. She seemed sufficiently to know the boundaries; and if she overstepped them, it was only to carry kindness.

"That's only the bad part of the story," I said; "now tell me the good part. There is always a good part to your stories."

She drove away the cloud at once, as well she might.   186

"Well, I went home and thought it over. I tried to think of myself in her position."

" Great heaven! "

" I admit that I did n't have much success, but the trying did me good. I saw that much of my feeling was due to mere tradition, to outrageous prejudice. I tried to forget that I had ever heard of such things before, and then asked myself what I ought to think. I did n't question any longer what I ought to do.

" I telegraphed to the Home. Though it was long past the time for her to reach there, they had not heard of her. I took the carriage and went down to the railroad station. No ticket had been sold to any one answering her description. About ten o'clock, I found her at the police station, — I had needed to give her only fifty cents for getting to the Home. She had been found in the corner of a warehouse porch, with her child in her arms, trying to snatch a little sleep. I cannot blame her for not wanting to go to the institution ; such places are so machine-like. I took her to my uncle's, and put her to bed. She became raving in her

187

sleep, and this afternoon I carried her to Mrs. Tamson's. When she gets well, I shall provide for her somehow."

" And what will the world say ? "

" It will say what it likes."

" Doubtless."

" I know that it 's a frightfully risky thing to meddle in such an affair ; but I can't help it. I won't be bound by a thing so utterly sense-less as the attitude people take in such matters. How can I possibly become contaminated by this girl ? I remember my wish that I could strangle Hilda, in Hawthorne's ' Marble Faun,' for her treatment of Miriam." A look of scorn came into her face. " What is such purity good for ? "

She stirred a little, nervously, in her chair.

" What is purity ? " she asked suddenly.

" It is a thing otherwise known by the name of Ruth."

She smiled gratefully.

" If that does n't suit you," I added, " I should rather trust your definition than my own."

I had long ago got beyond the stage of abstract definition of such things; with me they had become concrete. When I thought of them, I saw the face of Agnes, and latterly of Ruth; I had almost ceased to distinguish between mother and daughter.

After several moments of deep thought, she slowly answered her own question : —

"I should say that purity consists in avoiding everything that impinges on spiritual good. We ought to regard the word in a very broad sense. We restrict it too much; we attach it too much to accidents, and too little to the essence of things. There is hardly an action of life that may not be pure or impure. The spiritual must be pure; the material may be impure. Whatever use we make of the material side of us at the expense of the spiritual in any action of life is impure. Whatever use we make of the material side of us to benefit the spiritual is pure."

"I like that. I suspect that much of what the world calls pure would come under your definition as impure, and *vice versa;* but I like it so."

"Under my definition the girl across the way may be pure, though of course it is improbable. At any rate, I shall assume that she is, and I shall treat her as if I knew her to be so."

"Do you know," I said, "if I could have foreseen the advent of this girl just as she has come, I could have foretold your action? It is just like you, and every bit worthy of you, and you of it."

She smiled almost joyously.

A little later Harry came in with the morning's city papers. We fell to talking of the storm.

"By the way," said he, "have you heard about the man lost on Saddleback Mountain, — I believe they call it?"

Ruth turned to him breathlessly.

"No!" she exclaimed.

"He is a young scientist, Harris by name, who was trying to find some rare specimens of rock on the mountain. He went off this morning with his dog. At six o'clock the dog came whining home with blood on his hair, but without any visible bruise."

Ruth's face was white. She had risen while he talked. Her hand trembled on the back of her chair.

"Has anything been done?" she asked.

"There is talk of getting up a searching party."

"Are you going?" Her hand had become firm and her voice was clear, but she was still very white.

"I don't know; possibly."

"Will you go with me?"

"With you? Do you mean to go?"

"Yes; will you go?"

"Gladly."

"Do they know where he went?" she asked.

"Apparently not."

"Then I shall lead the way. Please go out and get eight or ten men to help me. I shall be ready in half an hour. Come to my uncle's house at that time. Can I count on you?"

"Assuredly."

Without another word she was gone.

Harry sank back in his chair as if the world had suddenly changed and he dreaded to face the new one.

"What does it mean?" he asked.

"I think it pretty evident what it means. She knows this man Harris, and cares very much about his safety. You have n't spoken to her yet, I take it."

He shook his head wearily.

"I don't know what to do now," he said musingly.

"I should think you had enough to do. If you don't hurry, you 'll keep her waiting."

An hour before, he would have given anything for the privilege of rendering her such a service. Now that he saw why the service was asked, his enthusiasm was gone. He went about his task with a fallen face. I was left alone to ponder and to wait for news.

Soon after they had gone the storm returned. The rain fell steadily, and the wind howled with hardly an intermission.

About midnight, under the plea of urgency, Harry was admitted to my room.

"Well, she found him," were his first words.

"Tell me all about it, — everything."

"I have n't had much time yet to think it over."

"I don't care to know what you think of it. I want facts."

"Yes, I suppose so. Well, I went out and found a group of men talking of getting up a searching party. I told them what Miss Appleton wanted to do, and said that she seemed to think she knew where to look for him. Most of them scouted the idea of a woman's leading such a party, especially at night. But one of them spoke up and said that he knew her, and guessed she could do anything she undertook. Another said he did n't know her, but knew enough about her to be willing to trust her common-sense. None of them had any notion where to look for the lost man, he said; and as Miss Appleton did, he was willing to try her. It resulted that they all agreed to follow her. There were ten of us.

"By this time it had begun to rain again, and the wind was springing up. As it grew worse, a few were inclined to back out, but the others hooted them. It was pitch dark when we gathered before Mr. Thomas's house, each with his lantern. In a few moments, a slight young man, with a big slouch hat drawn down to his ears, came out and asked if we were ready. The voice told the whole story. It was Miss Appleton. She had borrowed her uncle's shooting-suit throughout, even to the big corduroy trousers and top boots.

"In a very few words she told us what she intended to do. She told us where she thought the young man would be found, and asked us to correct her if she got upon the wrong track in trying to find the place. We were soon at the foot of the mountain. Then she took a compass in her hand, got her bearings carefully, and started into the woods straight away from the beaten paths. For half an hour we plodded on, — up over fallen tree-trunks, wet and slippery, down into ravines, under overhanging rocks, through dense bushes whose leaves emptied small showers of water upon us. She kept close watch of the compass, and would not swerve from the straight line.   She apologized for taking so hard a path by saying that in the pitch darkness it did n't pay to get off the correct line at all, for, if we did, it would be too hard to find the exact spot at the end.

"At last she came to a stop.   She told two men to go to the right about five rods, and look for a high cliff.   She told another two to go to the right five rods beyond the first two, and look out for the cliff.   She sent four more to the left in the same way.   All were to walk along parallel to our main line of march, measuring the distance, when in doubt, by calling every few minutes.   Pretty soon a man on the left shouted that he saw the cliff.   We all joined him.   Miss Appleton then told us that we were near the most dangerous spot on the mountain.   Beyond that cliff was a ravine with loose rock overhanging it.   A false step, or a heavy jar, or a fierce wind and rain might precipitate tons of rock upon our heads.   The lost man had gone into that ravine in the afternoon.   The storm had probably thrown down some of the rock upon him.   More was likely to fall at any moment.   She said she was going in there after him. She would not ask any of us to follow, because of the danger; but she wished those who did not go to remain just where they were. Without another word she started.

"Five of us followed. Then I saw why she had adopted man's dress. A woman's clothes would have been stripped from her in ten minutes. The ravine was full of huge stones, ragged, as they had been chipped off by the frost, and yet covered with water-soaked moss. We were continually slipping and falling upon these sharp points, so that our trousers were torn and our legs bruised. To make it worse, many dead pines had fallen into the ravine, across the rocks. The sharp stumps of their broken-off branches caught our feet and clothing, and tripped us unmercifully. A swift stream ran through the ravine. This was high and foaming. We often fell into it. On both sides of us, cliffs rose between fifty and a hundred feet, black and dripping. The rain fell in masses. The wind came in shrieking gusts. We would get well braced against it, and then it would suddenly stop, or shift, so suddenly sometimes that we lost balance. I never knew before what real wildness was like.

" Miss Appleton fell often, but was always up again with a spring. Her corduroys and heavy long boots withstood the assaults on them. She kept the lead. She peered into every nook and corner. Twice heavy rocks fell from a hundred feet above our heads and crashed down near us. We could hear the tearing of limbs above, the falling gravel, and then the crash near by. A small shower of dead trees followed. The ravine was so narrow that whatever fell was sure to fall in our path, — if not before or behind us, then upon us. For once I have tasted danger. Miss Appleton's face was always white; but she stopped only for a moment even when those crashes came.

" It was she who found him at last. He was lying unconscious in a hollow between two large rocks. One leg was sticking up along one of the rocks, and a small pine, evidently fallen from above, was lying across it. His head was bleeding. She rushed toward him, and tried alone

197

to lift the tree. We finally got him free, and carried him out to where we had left the other men. While we made a litter, she held his head close against her breast, bandaging the bleeding wound and putting brandy between his lips. Before we were ready to start, he was conscious. I never saw a man look so happy as he did when he realized where he was."

For several moments neither of us spoke; but I suspect that our thoughts were running along different lines.

"I believe I learned to-night what envy is," was Harry's final comment.

I must confess that I was not altogether free from it myself.

I suspect that even without it I should not have slept much that night.

XV.

THE doctors have at last told me what I have been so long prepared to know. It is strange that though a dozen years ago I should have been hardly moved by their words, now, at over seventy, I cannot think them other than cruel. Then I had nothing special to live for, and it would have been easy to die. Indeed, after Agnes had been lost to my outer life, I used to think that Fate had decreed the loss in order that I might be free from earthly ties, — might value my life cheaply. Of late I seem to have lost that freedom, — though, to be sure, it is but a trifling fragment of a life that I have to give or save. Ruth does not ask me to save it, — doubtless she does not want anything of it; but I would save it in the hope that it may serve her sometime. The doctors tell me that the injuries of the heart have proved too serious to overcome. Any day it may give up its task.

How can I wonder, after seventy years of faithful beating without a moment's rest!

I think that I shall tell Ruth and Harry today what the doctors have told me. It is strange that they happened to tell me so soon — only the second day — after the exploit on Saddleback. So much is crowded into these days! I wonder how much Ruth will care. She may not care at all for myself, but she will care because of my love for her. Her heart is so tender that it is touched by every other heart that it knows.

Harry did not come to see me yesterday. This morning he was looking disconsolate.

"How did you survive your adventure?" I asked.

"One part of it, the physical, I survived beautifully; the other part, as you can imagine, I survived not so well. Her treatment of the man she rescued broke me all up."

"Still, I suppose you realize that you can't complain."

"Certainly. She never encouraged me in the slightest degree. I fell in love with her almost at first sight, in Madawanipee; and long before you knew that I knew her she had put a quietus upon me several times, but I did n't know enough to know when I was beaten. I wish now that I had never seen the girl."

"I don't pity you a bit."

"I did n't suppose you did. You don't think me worthy of her."

"That is true; but I might pity you, nevertheless. When you say that you wish that you had never seen her, it is evident that you have already lost your love for her. A man does n't need pity for having lost a girl whom he does n't love."

"Don't, for Heaven's sake, talk that way! Can't a man regret his love for a girl?"

"Not unless something is wrong either with him or with her."

"I wish something would go wrong with the other fellow," he said, with forced gayety. "I 'd like to have him out of my way."

"It 's too late. What happened night before last showed that."

"I 'm not going to give up. I 'm going to

stay here and see her this morning. I see her on a little different footing here than elsewhere, and I 'm going to take advantage of it."

"Do you like to win with a handicap in your favor? I should think that you would be afraid of the time when she found out that the race was not fair at the start. But it makes no difference; for I can't let you stay this morning. I want particularly to see her alone. I wanted to talk with you on another matter; but you are in no mood for it, — or I 'm not."

It was with rather bad grace that he went away a few minutes later.

When Ruth came in, at eleven o'clock, she was even more cheerful than usual. It seems as if no shadow ever comes into her life; she is always cheerfulness itself. Perhaps it is because she lives deeply, and so knows the reality of the beauty of life.

"Your nephew thinks you very cruel this morning," she said, smiling.

"Have you seen him?"

"Yes; I met him half an hour or more ago."

"Do you think me cruel? I will make you my judge."

"I prefer to have no part in a judgment between you. Still," she added, "it does seem a bit hard to send away one who is ready to do anything that he can for you."

"Did you suppose that his eagerness to stay was due to eagerness to help me?"

"Why, of course."

This answer was accompanied by a smile which I confess is beyond my depth. I am so unready to interpret a woman's moods.

"Then you are not fit to judge between us," I said. "You would not see half the case."

"Justice is blind, they say."

"Blind to participants, not to facts."

"I must confess that I should be much more likely to be blind to facts. I should give judgment in your favor off-hand."

"How good you are to me! But was n't any part of your judgment in Harry's favor?"

"No; I could n't stop. He wanted me to go to walk with him, or boating or riding or anything, he said; but I told him I was in a hurry to see you, and could n't think of staying away so long."

She walked toward the window, picking up on the way a small satchel which she had laid on the table. She sat on the window-sill, and looked out in the direction of her uncle's house. After a long silence, which I dreaded to break with the news which I intended to tell her, she spoke very quietly : —

"I can see from here the house where we first met. I remember that night very well. I was reading when you came in. You spoke to me very kindly ; and something you said, or the way you said it, impressed me deeply. Strangely, I don't remember what it was. The story seemed very real to me ; but what you said made me look more carefully, young though I was, for the truly human element in everything I read. Partly through your suggestion, I came in time to see that the substance of human life is feeling, — that what we may not feel through our own experience we may feel through sympathy in the experience of others. My life has been richer since I appreciated that fact." 204

She paused a moment.

"You helped me again in Madawanipee. You showed your confidence in me. You had faith in my power to do good in the world, and that faith carried me through much which otherwise I fear that I should not have done. It helps me yet. I want to thank you for it all."

She was looking out upon the street again. It was several moments before she continued.

"To-day I have made, I think, a new discovery. You have told me something about my mother. But first, tell me, was there in High-bank any one else by the name of Alfred Robertson?"

"No; I was the only one."

I felt that she had discovered my secret. I had tried to avoid disclosing it, for it might seem to make a kind of claim upon her friendship. I regretted that she had even found it for herself. She might find sadness in it.

"And you loved my mother?" she asked slowly.

"Yes. But don't say loved, as if it were past and gone. I never ceased to love her."

She turned about and took a chair by my side. I put out a faded, wrinkled hand, and laid it open in her lap. She took it in both her strong, young ones. She moved as if to speak, but I interrupted her.

"You are your mother come back to earth again. Do you wonder that I have loved you so?"

She looked straight into my eyes without flushing or moving a muscle. I knew then that my faith in her had been justified. She had known my love, had taken it in the spirit of the offering, and had felt honored by it.

"I wish I were as worthy of it as my mother," was all she said.

Presently she took from the satchel an old, yellow letter, tender with age, and handed it to me.

"My mother usually destroyed her letters," she said.

CONCLUSION.

HERE the manuscript ended. The rest of Mr. Robertson's story I must tell from what I myself saw. He had admitted me to his adopted family, as he called it, on almost equal terms with Miss Appleton and his nephew.

One afternoon, in early fall, as I was approaching his room in my invalid's chair, Miss Appleton came out with frightened, sorrow-burdened face. She went down the corridor in the opposite direction without seeing me. When I entered the room, Mr. Robertson looked up painfully.

"Good-morning," he said; "she will be back in a moment. Won't you sit down and wait?"

He settled back into an easier position and closed his eyes, as if no further care was upon him. This was a new kind of reception. He had always been very cordial, heretofore. I sat down to await developments. In a few mo-

207

ments he opened his eyes, looked about as if just waking, and started up in a business-like way.

"Strange that she does n't come! I shall have to ring for her, and not keep you waiting."

"Whom do you mean?" I asked.

"Miss Appleton."

"I did n't come to see Miss Appleton. I came to see you."

"Oh, certainly, certainly!" he answered wearily. "Pardon me! What can I do for you this morning?"

"Nothing in particular, thank you. I thought perhaps I could read to you, — or do anything that you would like."

"You are very kind, but my secretary does everything. Good-morning!"

His mind was evidently wandering. He did not know me. It would be hardly safe to leave him alone, especially if, as was probable, there had been a change for the worse which the nurse had not seen. He tossed about nervously. At last he opened his eyes again, and recognized me. He held out his hand feebly, but with his usual cordiality of purpose.

After a few moments of conversation such as was usual with us, he took a fragment of an old yellow letter which lay beside him, and asked me to read it aloud. It read as follows: —

"I hope I am the first one to send you the news about Alfred Robertson. It ought to make you very glad. The mystery of the forgery has been cleared. You were justified in your confidence in his integrity. The pity is that you did n't dare to show it to him. The real culprit has confessed at last, after being caught in other forgeries in the West. You remember the forgery was a large check on a Western bank. I don't quite understand the process, but papa says Mr. Robertson, being a bank director, did not have to put his name on checks which he took to his bank to have cashed. It was said in the trial that he had dared to forge this check because he did n't think it could ever be traced back to him. Now it turns out that his secretary forged the check, and gave it to Mr. Robertson to cash. Then, afterward, the secretary got him to cash the genuine check also. This made the cash drawer 'over,' papa says, and the fellow put the amount of the 'over' into his own pocket. I don't believe I quite understand it, but I hope you will. You remember the sheet of practice paper that was brought into court. Every one said it was Mr. Robertson's practice work to forge the other name. Now it turns out that that rascally clerk had learned to copy Mr. Robertson's name exactly, and tried to change his writing gradually from one to the other. The signatures were a good deal alike. That was the evidence that counted most against Mr. Robertson. I suppose it was natural in face of it to believe the secretary's word sooner than his, in spite of his declaring his innocence. The rascal seems to have worked out his scheme very cleverly.

"And now, dear, I am going to step aside from 'minding my own business.' Will you be very angry if I mind yours a bit? Angie and Carrie and I were very sure that Mr. Robertson was in love with you, though he tried to hide it from everybody except you. Please don't be angry; but we thought you would some day, very soon, care for him. Then came that awful scandal about the forgery, and his conviction. You believed in him all the time, but I suppose you had n't come to love him quite. Then after his pardon he was afraid to carry the name of jail-bird to you, and he went away. I believe that even now, after the truth has come out, he would hardly like to make the first advance. He is so sensitive; and not everybody will have heard the truth. Why don't you write to him, and congratulate him on the triumph of the truth at last, and all that sort of thing? I suggest this for both your sakes."

Accompanying the letter was another, dated three days later, congratulating Miss Wentworth on her engagement. In it was this sentence: "It was strange that I happened to write to you about Alfred Robertson while the letter announcing your engagement to Mr. Appleton was on the way to me."

When I finished reading, Mr. Robertson's eyes were apparently fixed on the steeple of the Highbank First Church.

"I am glad she is n't going to marry him," he said, after a long silence.

I thought his mind was again wandering. He seemed to be thinking of the engagement noted in the letter of thirty years ago.

"Who?" I asked, hoping to recall him to his right mind.

"Ruth. Harry does n't deserve her."

He lay silent, as if in revery. Soon he began to talk again. I doubted, however, whether he remembered my presence; he appeared to be talking to himself.

"He does n't understand her," he said. "He lives in the world of sense; she lives in the world of ideas. He *must* not have her. I hope this man she loves is worthy of her."

Suddenly, after a few moments, in which an anxious look had played on his face, he smiled brightly, and spoke again. I moved my chair to remind him of my presence, but he did not seem to care.

"Strange how I forget myself! Here I have been worrying over Ruth's future. I have feared that she would make a mistake; but that

is as bad as Harry's fear the other night. I
scolded him for not having confidence in her.
How much more should I scold myself now!
She knows human nature. Other women may
make mistakes; she will not. If he is not
worthy of her, she will find it out; and she
will find it out in time. So instead of worrying, I rejoice. What do you think?" he asked,
turning to me.

"I should say that you have every reason for
rejoicing in her rather than worrying about her."

He lay still, with his eyes closed, for a long
time. He seemed to be breathing regularly;
and, as he had wandered but slightly, I saw no
necessity for summoning the nurses. I was not
familiar with sickness.

While glancing over a book which Miss
Appleton had left behind, I heard his voice
again. His eyes were open, but he seemed to
be looking into the distance.

"Yes; she kissed me," he murmured.

I stirred, and he looked up.

"Do you understand?" he asked, as if he
were trying to explain something.

"Yes," I answered, though I did not understand anything but the words.

"I hope you quite understand," he continued. "I fear you don't. She kissed me. Understand?"

I disliked to question, but I feared to miss any meaning which he wished me to get.

"Who kissed you?" I asked.

"Agnes, my Agnes, just now."

He turned again, and then suddenly put his hand to his forehead, and pushed back the hair. The natural light came back to his eyes.

"What did you say?" he asked.

"I did n't speak."

"Was it I who spoke last?"

"Yes."

"Oh, I know; I said that Agnes just kissed me. I was dreaming. It was Ruth who kissed me, just before she went out, when I told her that the doctor said that my time was short."

When he fell asleep again, I went to call a nurse. Miss Appleton returned with me. He was breathing heavily when we reached him. As we watched, his face brightened, and we caught a few words, uttered slowly, but cheerfully : —

" Ah, Life, you did not wholly cheat me — after all.   At the very end — the kiss of a woman — whom I loved."

He never spoke again.

THE END.

PRINTED BY JOHN WILSON AND SON CAMBRIDGE

215

www.ingramcontent.com/pod-product-compliance
Lightning Source LLC
Chambersburg PA
CBHW030326270326
41926CB00010B/1521